0056119

DATE DUE

DEC 0 4 1995	

E
99
N3
N375
1990

Newcomb, Franc
Johnson.

Navaho folk tales.

$10.95

NAVAHO
FOLK TALES

University of New Mexico Press　　　Albuquerque

NAVAHO
FOLK TALES

FRANC JOHNSON NEWCOMB

Foreword by Paul Zolbrod

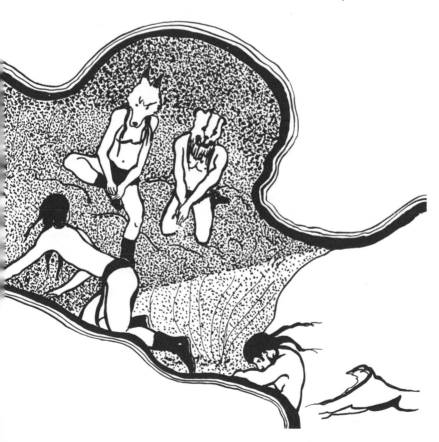

Library of Congress Cataloging-in-Publication Data

Newcomb, Franc Johnson.
Navaho folk tales / Franc Johnson Newcomb.
p.   cm.
Reprint. Originally published: Santa Fe, N.M.:
Museum of Navaho Ceremonial Art, 1967.
ISBN 0-8263-1231-4
1. Navajo Indians—Legends.
I. Title
E99.N3N375   1990
398.2'089972—dc20   90-39570
                                    CIP
                                    AC

In memory of
the late KENNETH E. FOSTER who
directed the Museum of
Navaho Ceremonial Art from
1955 to 1964

CONTENTS

FOREWORD

As SHE HERSELF INDICATES IN the introduction, Franc Newcomb originally assembled this volume of narratives for her children. However, that does not diminish their appeal to adults both with a desire to learn more about a Native American tribe and an appetite for literature at its classical best. Or so I would argue now.

The exploits of characters like Turkey and Snail function as viable paradigms of the epic heroism found in Homer or Virgil, even if the characters are animals. Recited with the kind of verve and affection found in *The Canterbury Tales*, they likewise convey the same kind of deep understanding of the human psyche Chaucer brings to his timeless narratives. These tales, when read carefully, capture the moment in Navajo prehistory when agriculture supplants hunting and gathering. Furthermore, the communication between beasts and mortals that prevails in such a primeval, albeit transcendently universal world, defines an accord among all living creatures that Western traditions scarcely preserve, unless we apply esoteric readings to such ancient works as the *Iliad* or the *Eumenides*, or learn to take the fables of Aesop more seriously.

I discovered *Navaho Folk Tales* quite by accident during the summer of 1969, while browsing through the books on display at the Museum of Navajo Ceremonial Art—as the Wheelwright Museum was then called. I had come to New Mexico looking for a viable precolumbian Native American poetic tradition, naively hoping to locate informants willing to recite old, unwritten stories for me. For religious as well as historical reasons, of course, that was not possible. Indeed, I had been rebuffed for expecting to recover material that way. If preliterate poetry still existed in the upper Rio Grande valley where tribal cultures remain fairly intact, it was probably too late to harvest any of it from the jealously guarded traditions of the Puebloan peoples. So I entered the Museum as a last gesture before leaving northern New Mexico, ready to give up my search altogether.

That is precisely when I found this work. Recalling one man's suggestion at Tesuque that the Navajos might more easily share material, I purchased a copy and began reading it at once. And at once it reinvigorated my original hunch that Native Americans produced significant poetry under conditions of preliteracy. Here indeed was a volume that displayed a new dimension to American literary tradition—a dimension totally overlooked among the print-driven Europeans who brought to the New World their scriptural religion and their bookish notions of poetry.

Converting what is written herein from traditional narratives, Newcomb produced a cohesive cycle of tales in a plain but eloquent idiom. The Navajos had obviously composed stories comparable with those of ancient Greece and Rome or postclassical Europe. The challenge I now recognized was to harvest additional material to strengthen that argument. Thus began my own effort to construct a comprehensive printed version of the Navajo Creation Story even more faithful to its tribal prototype.

At the time I even presumed that I could improve on what Newcomb had done. Yes, *Navaho Folk Tales* was extremely well-written, especially because of the crisp pace of its prose and its careful attention to details. But as I began to discover alternative accounts acquired by scholars like Washington Matthews or Father Berard Haile, and as I gathered additional information from older Navajos, I believed at first that what Newcomb had assembled was actually something of a simplified, bowdlerized version adapted exclusively for youngsters and squeamish Anglos. Somewhere in the array of Navajo ceremonial storytelling traditions there were fuller, more "adult" versions to be found.

Without an understanding of how such material functions in a tribal society where conditions of preliteracy remained strong, I initially took Newcomb somewhat too literally when she indicated in her introduction that she had gathered these tales "for storytelling at bedtime." There was a lightness in their tone that I misconstrued as prissy and evasive. This cycle did not acknowledge the overt sexual conflict and its monstrous consequences so important to earlier and seemingly more "authentic" retellings that I subsequently discovered. Nor did it contain the violence reflected in exploits like those of *Asdzani shash nadleehe*, Changing Bear Woman. Too much was missing; too much had been sanitized.

Studying it again on the occasion of its reissue, however, I am reminded of how shortsighted I had been in considering *Navaho Folk Tales* a curtailed account of the emergence. True, this work is not a "scholarly" version of the Navajo creation story. It may lack the documented comprehensiveness that I set out to attain, or the philosophical and ceremonial richness of the version that Leland Wyman assembled from transcriptions gathered earlier by Berard Haile. But such qualities may not really be as valuable as certain other features, like the flexibility within oral tradition that allows for youthful appeal in one telling and a more ponderous adult understanding in another; like a certain evasive archetypal unity that comes only with knowing all possible versions; or like a subtle merger of content and style that emerges from a storyteller's intimacy with the entire sprawling cycle no matter how he or she may choose to recite it any one time.

In a preliterate setting, a good narrative is elastic and adaptable. It may be presented as a composite suitable for a single telling, or it can be broken down into a series of individual stories told on different occasions. Segments can be isolated and expanded for different reasons, and any version can be refashioned some special way according to the storyteller's purpose and audience. If there is such a thing as an authentic text, that authenticity grows out of multiplicity and variation, not out of one particular version eclipsing all others. *War and Peace* does not have such elasticity, and if the *Odyssey* or *Beowulf* once did, that quality was lost when such works were transcribed and then outlived those who could recite them.

It is fortunate, then, that the University of New Mexico Press has elected to reissue *Navaho Folk Tales* and include it with publications like *Diné Bahane'*. As much as the latter, it deserves to stand with other printed Navajo accounts of the Navajo creation story. Once I learned to appreciate how incomplete any single version could be in the context of its vast preliterate network, I was worried that readers who knew literature only through print would think of it as the definitive version—the most authorative and the most complete. Indeed, as someone who originally expected to formulate a comprehensive text, I at first had to overcome such an insidious presumption myself.

This volume does away with such a notion, and does so very effectively, not only because its texture is so rich, but because it is at once so different and yet so intrinsically a part of some greater, unified whole. Where more emphasis falls on sexuality and male-female relationships in *Diné Bahane'*, for example, *Navaho Folk Tales* delineates relationships between animals and deities. Where in the former the trickster Coyote brings greater disorder, in the latter his adventures ultimately result beneficially. Where *Diné Bahane'* focuses more on defeating the rampaging alien monsters, in *Navaho Folk Tales* warfare is subordinated to agriculture. Turkey risks his life to bring seed corn to the fifth world, and the ants emerge with good, dry soil for planting them. Thus the animals help shape the fifth world. In the process it is explained how Turkey's tail feathers became blackened or why Snail carries his shell with him wherever he goes. If those explanations seem fanciful, not to be overlooked are the accurate generalizations they represent. Whoever first incorporated such explanations into stories observed features carefully and systematically, reflecting the deep human wonder that seeks to know why things are as they are, together with the poetic imagination that produces reasons. Such wonder is best transmitted to children under the stylistic conditions evident here.

Alike for lovers of great literature and students of southwestern Native American cultures this is an important book. We are beginning to learn how much genuine poetic material there is to be found in the upper Rio Grande basin and the Colorado plateau. At the same time we are discovering how much that material can teach us about the poetic process, to say nothing of the way the human imagination works in the vibrant setting of the oral tradition. The stories herein represent perhaps the oldest way of transmitting knowledge. Yet they open new doors of understanding and appreciation to readers who have always assumed that people can learn only from books.

Paul G. Zolbrod

FOREWORD TO THE FIRST EDITION

WHEN I HAD READ *Hosteen Klah: Navaho Medicine Man and Sand Painter,* the book written by Franc Johnson Newcomb and published in 1964, I had a feeling of deep regret as I turned the last page. I wanted her telling to go on and on.

It had been my good fortune to become acquainted with Mrs. Newcomb shortly after my arrival in the Southwest to attend the University of New Mexico. The talented lady then resided at their trading post home north of Gallup, New Mexico, but she was in great demand as a lecturer on Navaho culture, and frequently appeared in Albuquerque where I saw her from time to time. It was always a privilege to hear her talks and to see the fine collection of sandpainting reproductions about which she spoke and wrote.

Soon after having read *Hosteen Klah,* I met Mrs. Newcomb on a somber occasion in Santa Fe. Kenneth E. Foster had become acquainted with Mary Cabot Wheelwright, founder of the Museum of Navaho Ceremonial Art. In 1954 Miss Wheelwright engaged Mr. Foster to serve as acting curator of this institution, and he came to New Mexico to assume his new duties. A few months later, he was appointed to the position of curator, in addition to acting as secretary and treasurer of the Board of Trustees. He and Mrs. Newcomb became associates and friends.

Miss Wheelwright died on 29 July 1958 at her summer home in Maine. Until that time she had been the director of the Navaho Museum. At a subsequent meeting of the Board of Trustees, Mr. Foster was designated as the director. He held the position until 24 August 1964, when he suffered a sudden heart attack.

Mrs. Newcomb and I met, then, at a memorial service held for Mr. Foster at the Museum of Navaho Ceremonial Art. I had an opportunity to speak to the writer at that time, and I mentioned my feelings about her book. When I said that I had not wanted *Hosteen Klah* to come to an end, I also expressed the hope that other volumes were to follow. And Mrs. Newcomb assured me that she had another manuscript in press, and was working on a third.

The manuscript appeared as a second book, *Navaho Neighbors,* in 1966. Like its predecessor it was published by the University of Oklahoma Press.

Mrs. Newcomb, in telling of the third work, asked if I would prepare a foreword for it. The chosen title was *Navaho Folk Tales.* I was intrigued, and agreed to write the requested pages.

I had no idea then that in due course of time I would be selected by the Board of Trustees of the Navaho Museum to assume its directorship. When that action took place, however, I was delighted to learn of the possibility of bringing Mrs. Newcomb's latest book out under the sponsorship of this Museum, as its next hardback publication. Thus, not only have I had the pleasure of writing the foreword, but of bringing out another of Mrs. Newcomb's contributions to knowledge of Navaho culture.

I should like to explain the use of Navaho words. For many years, Navaho leaders implored the governmental officials not to use the Spanish spelling of the name by which they are usually designated today. They noted that they were in this region prior to the coming of the Spaniards, that they were *pre*-European Americans, and that they could see no excuse for spelling their name in other than the American way. Scholars have long done this; and at the Navaho Museum we follow this practice.

However, with actual Navaho words, the situation becomes more difficult. Originally, the Navaho language was unwritten. When investigators began recording data concerning the Navaho, their language was found to be complicated; and to record it required transcription characters not occurring in either the English or Spanish alphabets. It followed that each recorder set up his own scheme, or followed some orthographic system. Often the latter employs characters which ordinary typewriters or letter presses do not have.

One of the early recorders, Dr. Washington Matthews, made use of a certain system; Father Berard Haile started out with one manner of recording and later shifted to another; Dr. Gladys Reichard did relatively the same thing. Kluckhohn, Wyman, and their associates employed a recognized orthographic method—as did some of the others—but the characters are difficult to reproduce. Mrs. Newcomb adopted a useful way of transcribing her data; and Miss Wheelwright had her preferred style. Consequently, when one unfamiliar with the Navaho language encounters strange-appearing words, he is at a loss to know whether or not differing transcriptions apply to the same or disparate words, personages, places, and so on.

Here at the Museum of Navaho Ceremonial Art we are endeavoring to arrange a concordance wherein variations of the same word will be recorded. Insofar as is practicable, we shall use common terms in our publications, such as Spider Woman rather than the Navaho counterpart, *Na'ashjé'ii Asdzáán.*

Because a usable system of recording the Navaho language has been devised by Robert W. Young and put into circulation through published articles, books, and even newspapers, and because this system is readily available to us through the Bureau of Indian Affairs, we have adopted it. Accordingly, most of the Navaho words employed in *Navaho Folk Tales* follow this practice; and future publications of the Navaho Museum will follow this plan. Exceptions will be noted.

Mrs. Newcomb, as her books indicate, has used the spelling, *Hosteen,* when referring to a mature male person, whereas Miss Wheelwright preferred *Hasteen.* Mr. Young, who speaks Navaho fluently and has used it in all sections of the Navaho reservation, transcribes the same word as *Hastiin.* Certain divergences may be found in various locations, and one person hears the spoken word one way while another person hears it somewhat differently. Since we are publishing Mrs. Newcomb's current book, we are following the spelling *Hosteen,* as used in her previous publications.

On the other hand, we are adopting Mr. Young's spelling for that word which refers to the Navaho themselves, "the people," or *Dine'é.* This is easily typed or printed, and the pronunciation is clear. Almost every book or article treating of the Navaho gives this commonly used word in one spelling or another.

In preparing *Navaho Folk Tales* for the printer, Mrs. James W. Callaway devoted many hours to the editing and re-typing of Mrs. Newcomb's manuscript. Mrs. R. C. Alley, Jr., editor of *El Palacio,* read the work and provided editorial counseling. The original illustrations were drawn by Alfred Clah, a Navaho artist on the staff of our Museum.

With view to overseeing the Museum's program of publishing other books, and maintaining uniform style, spelling, and general practices therefor, I have given the manuscript its final editing. The sins of commission or omission are mine.

> Bertha P. Dutton
> Director
> Museum of Navaho Ceremonial Art

Santa Fe, New Mexico

INTRODUCTION

THE TALES RECOUNTED IN THIS volume were collected from various Navaho storytellers, with no idea that they would ever be presented to the public in book form. When my girls were small, and while we were living in our trading post on the Navaho reservation, I occasionally happened to overhear admonitions given them by the Navaho women who helped with the household tasks and the care of the children. I became aware that a wealth of folklore and folk sayings, common to every Navaho household, was being instilled gradually into ours. At one time I overheard She-ma say to Lynette, "Now don't you bother that spider! It will bring very bad luck if you kill it!" When I asked her why Navaho never kill spiders she replied, "Spiders are our friends! It was Mrs. Spider who taught the Navaho women how to spin fine threads of leaf fibers, cotton, and wool, and how to weave these threads into blankets and other useful articles. Then, too, it is Mrs. Spider who catches flies, mosquitoes and other flying insects in her web so they do not bother us. She has teeth sharp as needle points which slant backward so her prey has no chance to escape. If a child kills a spider, its second teeth will be crooked." And once I heard her say, "Oh! Don't step on that caterpillar! See how its hair moves along its back; if you kill it, your hair will all fall out!"

When I asked She-ma where these sayings came from, she told me they were parts of stories recited, in her family's firelit hogan during the long winter evenings, about the ancient days when animals and people spoke the same language and indulged in the same pursuits. It occurred to me that it might interest the children, and myself as well, to gather some of the tales for storytelling at bedtime. I knew that most of the Indians of our section were well versed in nature lore, and I imagined they could tell us many tales about the small animals, birds and insects with which they were familiar—stories we would find both unusual and amusing.

Before starting these folk tales, it may be well to describe the people and the area in which they live. The Navaho Indians, for the most part, are scattered over 16 million acres of land located in northwestern New Mexico, northeastern Arizona, and southwestern Utah. It is an area of mountains, upland plains, high plateaus, fertile valleys, deep canyons, and barren badlands. It has been called "the Land of Little Rain," but it probably receives as much or perhaps more rainfall than many other parts of the Southwest. The mountains are always green, with pine, spruce, Douglas fir, piñon, and juniper, while the high plains and mesas support growths of shrubs and grass. Even the semi-desert areas have their rainy seasons which fill the arroyos and swales with fresh water for varying lengths of time. Navaho sheep owners graze their flocks across the lowland areas during the winter months, and on the mountain sides or the high mesas during the heat of the summer.

Within the Navaho reservation are three prominent highland regions. Of these, Navaho Mountain, 10,416 feet above sea level, commands the extreme northwestern portion of Navaholand. It is a single peak rising five thousand feet above the surrounding plains. Black Mesa is located in the center of the reservation. Precipitous cliffs two thousand feet high outline the northern and eastern sides of this eminence, the circumference of which is about 250 miles; toward the southwest the land slopes gradually, with stream channels leading into very rough country. In the eastern part of the reservation, the Chuska-Carrizo mountain chain is made up of high, flat plateaus from which ridges and buttes rise to more than 9,500 feet. Locally known ranges, such as the Tohatchi mountains at the southern limit of the Chuska system, in New Mexico, and the Lukachukai, centrally located in this system in easternmost Arizona, figure in Navaho lore. Two rivers, the San Juan and the Little Colorado with small tributaries, drain the major parts of the reservation; both flow into the Rio Colorado. The entire region is crisscrossed with arroyos that carry raging torrents of water when storms occur on the mountain slopes.

The Navaho people do not think of the country as being either harsh or inhospitable. It is their "Promised Land" which they found after many long periods of migration. They have, of necessity, fitted their mode of life to its climate, its seasonal rains, the heat of summer and the winter sleet. Their thick-walled, dome-shaped houses, called *hogans,* are cool in summer and warm in winter. Even in the coldest weather, a small fire on the hogan floor keeps the dwelling comfortably warm. The smoke-hole in the roof provides ventilation; it is also a means of telling the time of day or night, for the sky serves the Navaho as a clock.

"Pesh-doclish Dezi," as we recorded it, was the Navaho name for the Newcomb Trading Post built at the point of Blue Mesa, where many Navaho families made their permanent home in sheltered spots along the sides of the mesa. These families, near or far, were our neighbors and made up the bulk of our trade, although customers came from a distance with teams and wagons to buy supplies that would last for a month or more, when again they would make the long trip to the post.

Our post was not only the center of community trade, but also the center of information concerning social functions and the exigencies of family life. We were always aware of family, clan, or community activities and were generally invited to participate. We were asked to attend weddings, rodeos, horse races and barbecues. It was not a far step from these forms of entertainment to their religious rites and ceremonials. I found the latter of great interest, especially when I discovered that each type of ceremony was founded on a long religious myth that explained its origin. The medicine men we knew were willing to relate them to us during the long evenings of midwinter. As these tales unfolded, the narrator oftentimes paused to explain the reason why some small insect, bird or animal was revered and protected by the Dine'é.

As my collection of tales recounted by She-ma was soon augmented by others from many other sources, it was not long before I realized that possibly half of them related to the creation story. Many began with the words, "In the beginning, when the world was new . . ." Others started with, "At the time when men and animals were all the same and spoke the same language . . ." It seemed appropriate, therefore, to arrange the tales in the sequence of the progression of Navaho emergence from the lower, First World, to the upper, or Fifth World, which is their present abode. Once collected, these ancient bits of folklore fell into an established pattern like bits of colored glass which, when correctly assembled, form the design of a stained glass window.

Although these Navaho folk tales parallel the creation story as they follow the lengendary history of the Navaho, they are, nevertheless, quite different in concept. They do begin with place and manner of existence by describing the First World as a small, dark place with no well-defined characteristics and with only a few inhabitants. Here I might mention that in all Navaho symbolism, darkness represents a place that cannot be seen and about which little is known. This First World was soon left behind and the people moved upward to a larger, brighter world. Then, as they progressed, each new habitation was larger than the previous one, and the inhabitants were more numerous. When they arrived at the Fourth World the characteristics of the country became quite definite, and many other peoples were mentioned.

The legends of all primitive peoples contain accounts of

great floods and also long periods of drouth and famine. In the Navaho tales four floods are mentioned, but only one that was said to cover the whole land. The "Great Flood" came after the Dine'é had become well established in the Fourth World, and it caused the greatest migration recorded in Navaho lore. Their manner of escape through a bamboo tree, which formed a ladder to the "Land Above the Sky," is purely symbolic. But many people have a certain tree which they consider sacred and revere as the "Tree of Life," so it is only logical that a tree, or reed, was chosen as the medium through which they gained access to the new world.

In all the myths, legends, and folklore of the Navaho storytellers, the direction of their moves has always been upward toward more light, a wider and more friendly land, and better living conditions.

It was during the period of life in the Fourth World that the myths and folk tales began to assume different characteristics. In the lengthy creation legends that have been collected by students of Navaho culture, the First People were dealt with collectively and received instructions from their deities; the importance of the individual contributor was seldom stressed. A few creatures such as the coyote, gopher, locust, and badger performed certain services, but many others were given no credit in the tales.

In these pages I have included the names and the deeds of many creatures whose activities were important to the First People. Among them are small Duck, Hosteen Snail, Green Frog, Crane, Packrat, Owl, and Bat who performed outstanding feats of valor, and whose stories I have related. There are still many untold tales in Navaholand. Almost any ancient storyteller, who desired to make his stories last through several long winter evenings around the hogan fire, could add forty or more names to this list, with an interesting tale for each. No two narrators ever agreed as to the exact details of these tellings, and often became quite unhappy when I suggested that both might be correct; for this reason I seldom took notes from two informants at the same time. I did record the names of sixty-three creatures that were permitted to use the tree as a passage to the Fifth World. I was told that each of these creatures was commanded to make some individual contribution to the general welfare, so I assume that there must have been, at one time, a tale about each of them. These tales may be mostly lost, or they may still be hoarded in the memory of some ancient Dine'é. In the past these folk tales were common knowledge and often repeated, as storytelling was the favorite form of evening entertainment. Although the ostensible purpose of these long nights of storytelling was to amuse whatever group gathered to listen, many of the tales were also for the purpose of instructing the young people in Navaho folkways and accepted social behavior.

One great law, emphasized over and over again, was that against killing. No bird, insect, animal or creature that had been allowed to ascend through the tree could ever be wantonly killed, nor could its flesh ever be used for food. It was believed that these forms of life had all been endowed with the same form of spiritual life as human beings and each had an equally important service to perform on this earth; thus they were treated with respect. This law still stands. It is seldom that a Navaho will kill a spider, an ant, a measuring worm or a squirrel, a bird, snake, bear, or any creature. The animals which the First People were permitted to hunt as game were those already inhabiting the Fifth World when the First People arrived. Later, some animals were created especially to serve as game, and they could be hunted at certain seasons of the year.

Navaho Folk Tales cannot be called a creation story, for no mention is made of a creator; nor does a continuous plan of action occur. Many inconsistencies will be noted. However, the tales present a glimpse of the stark beginnings of the Navaho, the struggles and hardships incidental to an urge to move upwards towards a better way of life, and the determination to carry with them all their hard-earned knowledge, leaving no creature, plant, or sacred mountain behind. Every man, animal, bird, or insect that made the difficult ascent to a higher domain was expected to bring with him some tangible magic, skill, asset, or knowledge which would be of assistance in making the new, uninhabited region into a place where all might live in comfort and harmony. It is the account of these individual contributions that furnishes the tales for this volume.

I should like to acknowledge my gratitude to those Navaho friends who related the folk tales that are published in this volume: Dudley DiJoli, Gleason Begay, Ahson Shema, Nah-toh Hathile, Hosteen Klah, Beaal Begay, Ahson Tsosie, and to others unnamed.

Sincere thanks are expressed to my daughter, Lynette Newcomb Wilson, who has aided me in compiling this work and who typed the original manuscript.

My hope is that all Navaho children, no matter where they may live, still have grandparents who enjoy relating these and other Navaho folk tales.

Franc Johnson Newcomb
Albuquerque, New Mexico

First Man and First Woman leaving the First World, the Place
of Running Pitch

Chapter 1

THE FIRST THREE WORLDS

NAVAHO STORYTELLERS OFTEN
start their tales with the beginning of time and with the lowest form of life in a place they call the First World. They all seem to agree that it was a dark place inhabited by crawling creatures, slugs, and larvae whose homes were holes in the ground, and where not even the insects had wings. In this lower world only a small area of solid land existed; it was bordered by pits filled with burning pitch from which came the only light. It was called the Black World, or the Place of Running Pitch. Not many people lived there and, as they were unhappy and miserable, they decided to move to a new world where conditions would be better and where everyone would have more room to move about.

"How can we leave this place?" inquired the ants. "Where will we go that will be any better? The rest of this world is burning and we cannot live there!"

Dragonfly answered, "We must have wings and we must fly to some other land." So Dragonfly made himself a double set of wings from thin, transparent mica and flew upward to the black dome of the sky. Locust saw how this was done and he, too, made wings with which to follow Dragonfly. Then all the others, the bees, the flies, the beetles, and even the ants tied wings to their shoulders and flew upward. Round and round they circled under the black dome, until Locust spied a faint blue light shining through a crack in the ceiling and called the others to follow him. The crack twisted and turned but they all squeezed through and finally found themselves in the Second World.

This place was blue and the light came from the blue sky that arched above the land. The land, too, was blue and extended as far as they could see in every direction. "We have reached a pleasant country," Locust announced, and all the others agreed, for there was grass on the ground and shrubs grew in many places. It was certainly a great improvement over the world they had left behind, and the land was so wide that each group could live by itself; community life had never been satisfactory even when the people were few.

Soon a large white crane came flying from the east, then a blue heron came from the south, a yellow grebe appeared from the west, and a black and white loon approached from the north. These big birds looked at the small insect people and said, "This is our land! You cannot live here! You must return at once to your own homes!"

To which Locust replied, "We cannot go back for our land is on fire and will soon be gone."

Then Crane said, "You cannot live here for there is no food in this part of the country. We birds have strong wings which carry us to the ocean that lies all around this land,

and that is where we get our food. But you will not be able to fly so far and you will starve."

Then the ants replied, "We can live on grass seed."

And Locust said, "We can live on the green leaves."

The bees and flies said, "We can live on the honey from the blossoms."

Dragonfly said, "I can live on the pollen."

When the big birds found that these new people did not intend to encroach on their food supply they said, "Stay as long as you please, but do not come near our homes." And, flapping their great wings, they flew away to the four corners of the Blue World.

The insect people built homes in the hard blue soil and stayed there a long time, until their numbers had increased so greatly that food was hard to find. The seeds and leaves had all been eaten and the pollen had blown away from the bulrushes and desert flowers. All were hungry and discontented. "We will leave this place and go to the land where the birds have their homes," they decided. So they unfolded their wings and rose in the air like a great dark cloud of wind-blown dust.

Now when the great birds who lived at the four corners of the world saw these clouds of insects approaching through the air they were greatly dismayed and said to each other, "These insect people must not come here to live! They will destroy all the grasses and the shrubs here as they have in the lands where they were living!"

The great, white Crane proclaimed, "We must declare war on all insects and drive them away before this happens. We will send messengers to all bird villages near and far asking for assistance."

The messengers were not gone long, and when they returned they brought with them all the warriors from the many colonies they had visited. Large birds and small came in troops and battalions to wage war against the Insect People. They all took their orders from the white Crane in the east, the blue Heron in the south, the yellow Grebe in the west, and the black Loon in the north and, so fierce was the battle, the insects were almost exterminated. When night came the ground was strewn with the bodies of those that had been slain.

Then Locust said, "We must flee while it is still dark, for this land will never be a safe place for us to live. The birds are our enemies and we must find a new country over which they do not rule."

So again the insects rose into the air and flew higher and higher until they reached the hard blue dome of the sky. There they circled round and round until they heard a voice from the south saying, "This way, this way!" It was the voice of the Blue Wind who had made a spiral passage through the sky and now led them to a new land on the upper side. Many of the birds that had been fighting them followed their trail through the opening and to this day are hunting and killing insects.

This Third, or Yellow, World was much larger and brighter than the Blue World had been, and standing in the four directions were high mountains, the crests of which gleamed brightly and lighted the whole land. Rivers ran in three directions and there were many springs of clear sweet water. Just as the Second World had been the home of the Bird People, this Third World seemed to be the home of all kinds of animals including human beings. There were trees on the mountains and plentiful grass and shrubs in the valleys, so the birds and the insects soon found comfortable places to live and all the food they needed. They made friends with the first inhabitants and for a while peace prevailed throughout the land. As the years passed and each group of people maintained its own activities and pattern of life, changes in their looks, habits, and characteristics began to take place. All remained about the same size, but it became possible to distinguish the humans from the lower animals, and the birds from the insects. They all spoke the same language, and they all had wings of various kinds. But the humans wore theirs attached to fur or feather coats so they could remove them when they were not in use. They had not learned to build houses but lived in caves or burrows along the hillsides, and their food consisted of seeds, nuts, berries, or roots which needed no cooking.

As the people increased in numbers their homes became crowded and, little by little, the supply of seeds, berries, and nuts on which they lived lessened so there was not enough for everyone, and only the strong and agile were well fed. Then neighbor fought neighbor; the packrat stole from the chipmunk, chipmunk stole from coyote, and the coyote stole from the mountain lion, so there was no peace in the land.

"We must do something about this!" said the humans and the other animals. "We must have a government to take charge of our affairs and to establish laws that everyone must obey," said the wisemen. "We must hold a council meeting," they all agreed.

Swift messengers were sent to ask all of the people of this Third World to attend a meeting where everyone would have a voice in deciding how the new government should be formed. Firefly was sent to the north, Locust to the east, Honeybee to the south, and Dragonfly to the west. As these four flew in straight lines, they would never be confused about the right direction. The meeting took place in a wide field where all the First People sat in a great circle and talked from dawn until sunset. Many plans were suggested for stopping the quarrels and for punishing the thieves, but no one knew how these plans could be enforced.

"We need someone in charge of community affairs," the people, the Dine'é, concluded, and all the others agreed. It was wise old Owl who blinked his eyes and said, "We need a leader, a headman, to rule us and keep everything in order. Then all this trouble will be ended."

"Yes, that is a good idea! We must have a headman," the others all agreed. "We must have a leader who will be strong and wise. Someone who will put a stop to all this quarreling and thievery."

In this circle of First People who had come to talk of forming a government were groups from four different places. On one side were the mountain people from the west; opposite them were the people from the high mesas and plains. At the south were assembled the people who had come from the fertile valleys, while the people of the forests had taken their places at the north. When it was agreed that they should have a leader, everyone began looking around to determine whom they might choose who would be strong, and just, and wise, and kind. The mountain people finally said that they had chosen Mountain Lion because of his strength and wisdom, but many others were not pleased with this choice. The people of the plains suggested that big Wolf, who also was strong and quite famous for his cunning, should be given the leadership. But this suggestion did not please the others any better than the first. A spokesman for the people from the forest arose and said that Hummingbird could fly very swiftly from place to place to learn where crimes were being committed and to apprehend the wrong-doers. To this, many others objected and said that Hummingbird was much too small to be their ruler. The people who had their homes in the fertile valleys made their choice saying, "Bluebird is a very wise person who makes friends and brings good luck and happiness wherever he goes. We would like him for our leader." The others would not agree to this and they said, "Bluebird is too kind to punish anyone and if he were headman we would be no better off than before." Then no one knew what to do about selecting a leader until wise Owl told this plan:

"Lion, Wolf, Hummingbird, and Bluebird have been named as being strong, cunning, swift, and kind. Of these we do not know whom it would be best to choose for our leader. So let the four go to the edges of the world and bring back something that will be useful to all of us. The one who brings back the most useful thing shall be our headman."

"That is a very good plan," agreed all the people. "Let the four go in different directions and see what each can find that will be of benefit to all of us."

The four chosen candidates were very glad to travel afar to discover what might be found at the ends of the world, and immediately started making preparations for the long journey. First they filled bags with food and jugs with water, then they braided their hair with strips of red willow, painted their bodies white with red clay stripes, and last of all put travelers' moccasins made of yucca strands on their feet. When all this had been done, Wolf started toward the east, Lion to the west, Hummingbird flew northward, and Bluebird journeyed south. For eight days and nights the First People chanted prayers and waited for the return of the travelers. On the morning of the ninth day, as light was filling the eastern sky, they saw Wolf walking toward them, dressed in such shining garments that they hardly knew him. On his head was a gleaming white cloud, while his body was wrapped in a beautiful white robe made of eagle feathers. In one hand he carried a white gourd rain-rattle and in the other a stalk of white corn.

"What are these things you are bringing to us?" all the people asked as he came inside the circle.

"I bring morning light, spring showers and young corn!" replied Wolf. "These are the things I found on the eastern mountains." Now, when the First People saw how grandly he was dressed and had examined the wonderful things he had brought, they looked at each other and said, "Surely no one could bring us anything better than this! We will make him our leader, and then we can go back to our homes; there is no need to wait for any of the others."

So they appointed Wolf to be their leader, and he gave them the gifts he had brought from the east.

Before they had completed this ceremony, someone pointed to the south and everyone looked in that direction.

They saw Bluebird coming toward them dressed in such fine clothing that he appeared as a stranger. He wore a beautiful robe made of blue beads, and on his head sat a bright blue cloud. In his right hand he carried a rattle made of blue turquoise and in his left was a stalk of blue corn. All the people gathered around him to ask, "What are these things you have found in the south?"

And Bluebird replied, "I bring you blue sky, summer rain, and soft corn."

The people looked from Bluebird to Wolf and back again, saying to each other, "Bluebird has brought gifts that are every bit as useful as those brought by Wolf! Now what shall we do about this? We cannot throw these things away!"

"Perhaps we can have two headmen," remarked wise Owl. "After all, two leaders could watch over us better than one."

The others thought this would be a very good way to settle the matter, so they told Bluebird that he and Wolf were both to rule because they had brought gifts of equal importance to all the First People.

It was now agreed that everyone would await the return of the other two travelers, and soon Lion was seen approaching from the west. He, too, was dressed so magnificently that everyone marveled at his grandeur. The yellow robe across his shoulders was made of canary feathers and a yellow cloud stood on his head. In his right hand he was holding a rattle made of jasper, while in his left hand was a stalk of yellow corn. As he walked into the circle of waiting people they all explained, "What are you bringing? What did you find in the west?"

"I have evening light, autumn rain, and ripe corn," replied Lion. Now these were all things the First People would need if they were to have good harvests and food to store for the long months of winter. They knew that these gifts which Lion had brought were just as necessary as those that had been given them by the other two.

"There is only one thing we can do about it," remarked
Owl. "We will make him a leader also."

So they accepted his offerings and told him that he was
to reign along with Wolf and Bluebird. The yellow afternoon sunshine was slanting across the land and Bat said,
"The sun is too bright, it is hurting my eyes."

Blind Mole agreed with him, and the two left the circle,
Bat going to his cave and Mole to his burrow. Coyote also
had become weary of waiting, as this was the time of day he
usually searched for his food, and he said, "We now have
three leaders and that is enough for any people. They have
brought us gifts that will supply all our needs, so let us go
to our homes and not wait here any longer."

But he had no more than said this when Hummingbird
could be seen approaching from the north. His robe was
even more dazzling than those worn by the other three, for
it was woven of all the colors of the northern lights. On his
head he wore a cloud of rosy mist, while in his right hand
he carried a deep abalone shell bowl filled with beans of
many colors, and in his left, a dry stalk of variegated corn.
As soon as he stepped inside the waiting circle, they inquired, "What are the presents you have brought to us from
the north?"

Then Hummingbird replied, "I have brought northern
lights for the dark days of winter, and I have brought you
all kinds of stored corn and beans for your winter's food.
This bowl can be used for storage and it will never become
empty."

The First People knew they would need these things as
much as they needed the gifts of the first three. Even though
Hummingbird was small, he had brought gifts of equal importance to those brought by Wolf, Bluebird, and Lion. So
it did not take the First People long to decide that Hummingbird must also be appointed a leader. They told him
they were glad he had brought such wonderful and useful
gifts, and now he, with the other three, would reign over

the land. Because they had appointed four headmen to rule over the land, the First People decided to give them the title of judges. That is how it came about that the Dine'é have never been ruled by a chieftain, but have always been governed by a group of wisemen who call the people together for council meetings when community problems are to be solved.

To this day the lion wears a yellow robe, the bluebird has a coat of blue feathers, the wolf's is silvery white, and the hummingbird wears a coat of many colors. They wear these to remind the people of the gifts they brought from the ends of the earth, while all were living in the Third World.

Hosteen Coyote gambling with the First People while they dwelt in the
Fourth World—a dice game

Chapter 2

THE FOURTH WORLD

FOR A TIME ALL WENT WELL
with the inhabitants of the Third World. They had more
light than in the land below, though the dim yellow fog
gave them neither night nor day.

But when the four travelers had brought farm seeds to
the First People, they had not stayed with the donors long
enough to learn anything about the corn or the beans or
other farm plants, and they had not taken the trouble to
learn the prayers and rites to bless the seeds and the fields
before the planting took place.

When it came time to plant the fields, one said to another, "Tell me how this corn should be planted." And another said, "Tell me how these beans should be planted." But no one knew how it should be done.

"We will plant them as the wind plants the grass seeds," they decided. So they loosened the soil in their fields and scattered the seeds over the top, then asked the south wind to cover them with dust, and the rain to fall from the clouds and moisten the dust.

Unfortunately, the seeds were so near the surface of the ground that when they started to sprout, the cutworms and the beetles destroyed many of them and, when the ears started to form, grasshoppers and crickets ruined still more. Then when the kernels were in the milk all the First People stopped gathering seeds and nuts and began to live on corn and green beans; very little was left to ripen for the next planting. The next season the fields were smaller and the corn plants did not produce many ears. After several planting seasons had passed, the seed was all wormy and not a stalk of corn grew in any cornfield. Once again the First People were forced to wander near and far searching for food which was never plentiful, and it seemed that they were always hungry. Again quarrels broke out and they stole from each other whenever an opportunity arose. Neighbors became bitter enemies over a little patch of grain, and no one was happy.

The four judges decided that something must be done, so they sent messengers in all directions to call the people to a council meeting. A great assemblage of the clans took place on the appointed day, for a most important decision had to be made. When the people of the fertile valleys had told of the scarcity of grain and sunflower seeds, the people of the lakes had mentioned a dearth of rice and lily-bulbs, and the people of the forests had voiced complaints about the scarcity of nuts and acorns, it was decided that all the

First People must leave this place and find a better world in which to make their homes.

When this decision had been reached and agreed upon by all present, the First People put on their winged suits and flew to the sky. Here they circled widely, searching for an opening that would lead them to the land above, but they found nothing except the hard smooth surface with no holes or cracks anywhere. They were becoming tired and discouraged when suddenly they heard a voice coming from the east saying, "This way! Come this way," and looking in that direction they were surprised to see a blue-masked face peering at them over the edge of the sky. Just at that moment a voice came from the south saying, "Come this way! This is the way to the upper world." Then a voice from the west said, "Come this way." And a voice from the north said the same thing.

The voices were coming from the masked faces of First Woman in the east, First Girl in the south, First Man in the west, and First Boy in the north. These four were trying to show the travelers the way to the Fourth World which spread its mountains and its rivers so far above the land in which they had been living.

The mass of air-borne people then divided into four groups and flew toward the four voices. Those who were to be the First Dine'é flew to the east and followed First Woman to the upper side of the sky, and that is why she has always been in charge of their welfare. The Bird People heeded the call of First Girl and flew to the south where she led them upward to a new land, and that is why many birds still fly to the south to escape the cold months of winter. The Animal People went to the west where First Man was calling, and when they reached the upper world they found themselves surrounded by high mountains, and there they have made their homes to this very day. It was then that the rule, or law, that only men would be permitted to hunt wild game was established. All the insects and crawlers flew to the north where First Boy had been calling, and when they arrived in the new world, it was so cold that they immediately crawled into holes or made themselves burrows in the earth where they huddled together for warmth. That is why most of them now hibernate or wrap themselves in warm cocoons during the winter months.

When all had finally scrambled over the edges of the sky to enter the new world, they gathered in four groups to look around and discover what sort of place they had found. What was their surprise to see people on every side of them! There were the Hopi and other Pueblo Indians who wore their hair in bangs that came to their eyebrows; there were the Ute and the Comanche whose long braids, ornamented with feathers and porcupine quills, hung over their shoulders; some had shaved their heads until only one long lock of hair was left at the very top; and still others had locks cut straight across at shoulder length.

The Dine'é had never cut their hair into particular shapes or patterns. Their long black locks were combed straight back from their foreheads and tied in double loops at the back of the head. Men and women wore the same type of hair-do.

A great many strangers appeared in the Fourth World; however, the first four people who had called to them were Dine'é like themselves, and they now gave orders to the new arrivals. First Man said to the animals, "You will find homes among the trees and rocks of the mountains to the west." First Girl said to the Bird People, "You will have your homes in the sunny land of the south."

The Insect People had already found homes in the earth, so First Woman spoke to the Dine'é who were grouped in the east saying, "Where have you been living all this time? You are dirty and you smell badly! Have you been living in dens with the badgers, or in some abandoned owl's nest? Go and bathe yourselves, wash your hair, and eat no food until I see you in the morning."

First Man and First Woman, with several children, had come to this Fourth World a long time before these later people had arrived. They found that it, the Black-and-white World, was much brighter than the Third World had been; here was light during the day. The plants grew faster, seeds and berries ripened sooner, and edible roots grew larger. Beside these foods, the First People had corn and beans for the first time. It was no longer difficult for the wisemen to preserve order, for all who cared to work could, and they could have all the food they needed.

By the time the latecomers reached the Fourth World, First Man and First Woman had been living with the Pueblo Indians long enough to have acquired much of their advanced culture. They were glad to welcome their own people, yet they were ashamed of their appearance, for some were dressed in strips of hide while others wore capes of feathers. Their long black locks hung below their shoulders, and no one wore moccasins or leggings. First Woman showed them how to roll their hair into double loops at the back of the head and how to bind it there with white cotton cords. The older Navaho men and women tie their hair in this fashion to this very day.

As the newcomers looked around, they saw high mountain peaks covered with green trees on all four sides, and stone houses with walled patios near them. Below them were fields of corn irrigated from running streams. This was something they did not know about, and to them it appeared as though the corn was growing in a pond or marsh. First Woman said to them, "If you are going to live here you will have to learn how to raise corn."

"But how will we learn, and how will we get the seeds?" asked the newcomers.

"You must make your homes near the Pueblo peoples. You must work in their fields as farm laborers," she replied. "Then you can earn your food and also earn the seeds to plant in your own fields."

While they were still talking about this they noticed two columns of whirling dust approaching, one from the north and the other from the south, each carrying something that resembled grey tumbleweed at its base. Suddenly the two dust columns came together with a loud noise, then rose up and disappeared in the sky. Where they had met there stood two people with dusty, grey coats; one was Coyote and the other was Badger. Because of this miraculous birth, these two are said to be cousins of the immortals.

"Look what the north wind has brought us," said First Man. "It has brought us laziness and trickery."

"Look what the south wind has brought us," said First Woman. "It has brought us industry and perseverance." And to this day these are thought to be the qualities of Coyote and Badger. By this time Badger had started digging a hole in the hillside where he wished to make his home, while Coyote had wandered away to see what he could find around the homes of the Pueblos, thinking that if Badger built a warm comfortable home, he would share it without the bother of building one for himself.

After First Man and First Woman left them, the people talked a long time about how they might be able to obtain food. Some wished to go to the Pueblos immediately, but others wished to wait awhile as there were plenty of seeds, roots, and berries where they were, and they did not need corn just yet. While they were talking, Coyote hid nearby and listened to their arguments. Finally he stepped to the center of the circle and said, "You need not work for the Pueblos to obtain your seed corn! I have been there and have seen how the fields, with their rows of corn, stretch up and down the river bank. There is no one to guard them and no one to prevent us from taking all we need."

When the First People heard this a great hubbub arose, as property rights had always been strictly observed by their members and they were afraid that some great evil might come to them if they stole from their neighbors. When this was explained to Coyote he said, "The stalks are tall and each one bears twelve ears and just as many leaves. If one ear is taken from the bottom of each stalk the Pueblos will never miss it."

The First People began to think that this would be an easy way to obtain the corn they needed for planting, and it would certainly be much quicker than working for it. So when Coyote said he would go to the east if volunteers would go in the other three directions, they decided to accept his plan.

Mrs. Spider wove sacks for each one to take and the four started off. Coyote went to the east, Skunk went to the west, Magpie flew to the north, and Crow winged his way toward the south. The Pueblo cornfields were some distance away, so the four would travel all day, pluck the corn at night while it was too dark for the Pueblos to discover the thieves at work, and then return in the early dawn. The people waited through the night and when dawn-light streaked the eastern sky, they saw Coyote approaching, carrying a heavy sack. "Here comes Coyote," they cried, "make a place for Coyote!"

Coyote stepped into the circle, but he did not seem very happy. "Open your sack and pour the ears on the ground," they told him. So Coyote opened his sack and spread the corn he had brought where all could see. As the First People examined these ears, it was plain to everyone that they would never do for seed as they had been growing so low on the stalk that the irrigation water had soaked through the husks and had made the kernels soft and mushy. The people were disappointed but said to each other, "The others will bring good corn."

Skunk was next to make his appearance, with his sack only half filled. "This was all I could get," he told the people. "The ears were too far from the ground for me to reach them." Then he opened his sack and emptied the con-

17

tents where all could see. The ears were large and ripe, but field mice had gnawed the germ from every kernel except the tiny ones at the tip. Nothing was left that was worth planting.

This was indeed a disappointment to the people who were planning to have wide fields of corn. Now only Magpie and Crow remained to bring all the seed for everyone. It was not long until Magpie came flying from the north. Her sack was filled to the brim, but when the ears were spread on the ground it was plain to all that they were not worth planting, for Magpie had sat on the tip of each corn stalk to pick the tiny nubbins that grew near the tassel, and most of them were full of worms. This was not the kind of corn the Dine'é could use for seed.

Now the people waited for Crow to appear from the south, and after a time they saw someone coming slowly toward them, but it did not look much like Hosteen Crow. When he had left them, he had been wearing a silver-grey coat and white vest and white leggings, but this person was entirely black, down to the tips of his tail feathers. Even the sack which had been silvery-grey was now a dingy black.

"What happened to you? What happened to you?" the people all cried at the same time. But Crow only shook his head as he spread the ears from his sack on the ground.

"They caught me and painted my coat with corn smut," he croaked. "They filled my eyes and my mouth too, so I could hardly see where I was going. They dragged my sack around and filled it with the poorest corn they could find."

Sure enough! The ears from his sack were black with corn smut and mold, so none could be planted. Crow flew away to try to clean the black smut from his feathers, but it never came off and he was worn a coat of black ever since.

Now the First People realized they had been wrong to act on the advice of Hosteen Coyote instead of doing as First Woman had bidden them. They decided that if they were to obtain farm seeds from the Pueblos, they must work for them; they also agreed that the seed would be of little benefit unless they learned from the Pueblos how to prepare the fields, when and how to plant the seeds, and the prayers that must accompany this work. A council was held in which First Woman was the speaker. She said, "A maiden must be sent to each pueblo carrying gifts to exchange for seeds, and a youth must accompany her to work on the farms of each village in order to learn the planting rites and the prayer chants that accompany them." This seemed like good advice and the people looked around to find eight young people who would be willing to go on this mission.

"I will go!" volunteeered Otter's daughter. "And I will give them my white shell bracelets." She held up twelve white shell bracelets for all to see.

Then her brother said, "I will go with her to learn the planting rites and the Seed-blessing Ceremony." Then these two started toward the east.

"I will go!" exclaimed Bluebird Maiden. "And I will give them my turquoise amulet," and she held up a large, oddly-shaped piece of turquoise.

"I will go with her," said Mockingbird Youth, "to learn the Corn-blessing songs," and these two started toward the south.

The next to speak was little Canary. "I will go," she offered, "and take them my bowl of yellow pollen." She held up a bowl made of yellow jasper which was filled with sunflower pollen.

"And I will go with her," said the yellow-shouldered Blackbird, "to learn the Growing Ceremony." They departed toward the yellow mountains in the west.

"I will go north and give the Pueblo farmers the pink coral beads I wear around my neck," stated Beaver Girl as she held up the beads where all could see.

"And I will go with her," said Muskrat Youth, "to learn the Harvest Ceremony;" and these two started the long journey to the north.

The First People knew it would be a long time before
the eight emissaries would return, so they went to the valley
to prepare their fields, leaving only four watchers on the
mesa to warn them of the youths' return. It was late in the
planting season when Otter Girl was seen approaching from
the east. In one hand she carried a basket of white corn and
in the other, three stalks of beeweed. Then from the south
came Bluebird Maiden bringing a basket of blue corn and
three vines of different kinds of beans. From the west
Canary Girl appeared bringing yellow corn and vines of
squash, pumpkin, and melons, and last to arrive was Beaver
Maiden with her basket filled with variegated corn, and in
her left hand, three stalks of tobacco and other healing herbs.
The First People were very happy to have all these things to
plant in their fields, and they made a rule that from then on
all seeds would belong forever to the women, who should
save them during the winter and plant them in the spring.
This law is still observed and Navaho women plant the seeds
in the fields that have been prepared and furrowed by the
men.

The four youths had been told by the Pueblos to stay
nine days and nine nights after the maidens had departed. In
that time they would be taught all the ceremonies that
should accompany planting and harvesting, so the First
People stayed where they were to await their return.

The youths came from the four directions at the same
time, and all were carrying rain-rattles and elaborate medicine bundles. All wore ceremonial garb with feather headdresses, red leather moccasins, and arm bands that had been
given them by their instructors. They were now medicine
men, or singers, who could hold all the rites of seed blessing,
planting, and harvesting. From that time nearly all medicine
chanters have been men.

The fields that had been prepared were now quickly
planted, irrigation ditches were opened to bring streams of
water, and the farms of the Dine'é were almost as extensive

as those of the Pueblo peoples. The plants grew rapidly and the harvest ripened quickly, so it was not long until the First People had more food than they could use. It was no longer necessary to walk on the hillsides gathering berries, as plenty of melons grew in the fields; and no one needed to harvest wild grains or sunflower seed when they had an abundance of corn and beans. Between the periods of planting and harvesting little work was to be done, so the First People started playing games which they had learned from the Pueblos who were great gamblers. The women played games of chance with smooth stones and flat sticks that were black on one side and white on the other, and the men amused themselves with wooden dice.

These games were played by small groups of gamblers, and when one person was especially lucky he would continue as long as his luck was good. After a time it became apparent that Hosteen Coyote was the lucky player and no one could win from him, so no one would play with him or make a bet against him. As each gambler made his own dice, Coyote had found a way to insert small bits of obsidian into his dice making them heavy on one side, and for that reason he could always win.

When his own people refused to play with him, Coyote sent word to the Pueblos that he would like to compete with their best players in a game of dice. Now the people of the pueblos had been playing this game a very long time; they had many skilled players who seldom lost a game. They were sure they knew how to prevent Hosteen Coyote from cheating even though his dice were weighted. Their plan was to have him exchange dice with his opponents as the game progressed so that he was seldom using his own dice. But Coyote made ready for these rules of play by making two sets of dice, one weighted so the winning side would fall upward and the other weighted so the losing side would appear. Hiding one set in his fur collar, he placed the other in his carrying bag where all could see. He was ready when invited to come to the place the Pueblos held their games.

The games arena was a circular patio surrounded by a high wall near the home of Water Monster, who had been chosen to be Coyote's opponent. The two players removed their fur coats and placed them on a stone bench that stood against the wall; they then placed their bets with the judges and sat on the adobe floor to begin the play. Before the first throw, Coyote was asked to exchange dice with Water Monster, so he brought fourth the dice that would always lose, and handed them to his opponent. For a while they played and Coyote won all the bets, then the director again asked them to exchange dice, so Coyote gave up the ones he had been using and took from his fur the ones that would always win. So again he was lucky and his winnings made a great pile of valuables on the patio floor. Four times the director asked for a change of dice but it made no difference in Coyote's luck, and finally Water Monster had nothing to bet except his fine fur coat.

"One more game and I am through," Water Monster stated, "but I think there is something very queer about all this!" The last game was played with the usual result, and Coyote gathered his winnings into his carrying bag, then went over to the wall and picked up the two fur coats. He hurried away and ran home as fast as he could, for the Pueblos were very angry when they saw him taking so many valuable things from their villages. Coyote put everything into a hidden storeroom, but he did not know until he started to hang it on a peg in the wall that an inner pocket of Water Monster's fur coat held two tiny Water Babies. These Water Babies were so small that they slept all the time and made no outcry, so Coyote decided to keep them and not tell anyone he had them.

Coyote's trickery resulted in a great flood which forced the First People to leave their pleasant Fourth World

Chapter 3

THE FLOOD

DURING THE TIME THE FIRST People had been living in the pleasant Fourth World, they never thought that some day they would be obliged to leave, and with so little warning that most of their possessions would have to be abandoned. They little dreamed that they ever would be driven from their homes by the angry waters of a great flood.

But Water Monster, reaching his home in the evening, learned that his babies had been stolen. When he found they were gone, he flew into a terrible rage and shouted that he would destroy all the people who lived in that land, and then he would destroy all the land on which they lived. Diving to the bottom of the ocean, he opened all the flood gates that had kept the lower waters from boiling up into the ocean, and soon all the water that had been stored in the caverns under the earth came spouting out of these lower depths.

At first the waters of the ocean rose slowly and evenly over the edges of the land, covering the lowlands and then creeping higher and higher. But soon a fierce wind started blowing and the water raged over the land in great foam-covered waves. This made a wall of water many feet high all around the land, and the foam-covered crest could be seen a long distance inland. The water rose higher than the tallest mountain peaks.

Finally the people, in an effort to reach the land above the sky, were forced to seek an opening in the turquoise dome that arched above their abode. They had found in this Fourth World everything they needed to make life comfortable and happy. This was a summer land where little change in the seasons occurred, and warmth came from the earth and the sky. The people had no need for protection against cold winter storms, so their homes were often no more than crude brush shelters built near their cornfields, close by springs of clear water.

After the fields were planted, they required little care until harvest time, when the First People gathered melons, squash, pumpkins, sunflower heads, rice, corn and beans to feed everyone until the next harvest. They believed that they had reached the end of their travels and that this was the Promised Land of their dreams.

In this land the First People had increased until thirty-two clans were counted. Each clan, made up of several families, had its own dwellings and its own farms. The head clanswoman chose the place where she wished to live and, then, her clan would be named from some special feature of that place, such as "White Water," "Striped Rock," "Red Earth," and so on.

The people worked their fields in the daytime, then danced, sang, and told stories in the evenings. In each clan an elder one, known to be a wiseman, established the rules of conduct for all members of his clan. When community problems arose, the thirty-two wisemen would meet to discuss matters and to reach a decision that would be fair to everyone. Most of the First People lived in peace with their neighbors and quarrels did not occur.

The only two who made any trouble were Coyote and Packrat. Coyote played tricks on everyone; putting tiny yellow stones in the corn which the maidens were grinding for meal so that it was gritty and full of sand; making small holes in the bottoms of the water jars so the water all dripped out as it was being brought from the spring; and gnawing the heads from the sunflower stalks so there would be no seeds to gather for food. Packrat was not a trickster, but he was a thief and, although he was frequently punished, he could never resist stealing ears of corn from his neighbors' cornpits, or carrying away long strips of pumpkin and squash that were drying on the bushes. It is true that he always left something to take the place of the things he had stolen, but the burdock burrs and the empty milkweed pods he put in their place were of no use to anyone. Whenever these depredations became unbearable, the clan elders were called upon to punish the offenders, and this they did by sending them on long, tiresome journeys to bring news from the Pueblo villages.

During all these years of prosperity, Turkey had lived with the family of First Man and First Woman as a pampered pet. He did not care to fly away to the tree-covered mountains or to the high mesas because, at the side of their home, they had built for him a nice wicker house with a lattice door; they had given him a pottery water bowl, a stone food platter from which to eat his corn, and had placed a strong juniper pole in his house where he could roost at night. In return for all this he was willing to give First Woman the soft downy feathers from his breast to weave into feather blankets so she and her family would have warm covers when the nights were cold. To keep Turkey from becoming discontented and running away, First Woman gave him all the food he could eat. She gave him corn and wild millet, seeds of squash, melons and sunflowers, and even bean sprouts. As Turkey was very fond of good things to eat, he soon grew large and fat and very short of breath, so when he walked fast or ran for any distance he became quite red in the face. When it came to flying, his wings had lost their strength, so they could hardly lift his body off the ground. For this reason he never tried to fly, and he very seldom attempted to run; eventually he became so lazy that he did very little except strut around and act like the most important member of the family. Occasionally, when he was tired of a diet of seeds, he would wander through the cornfields searching for grasshoppers and corn beetles as a change. Sometimes he would take long walks with First Woman's small son along the grassy hillsides or on top of some high mesa. From this point of vantage they could see the land stretching out in three directions to meet the dim line of the horizon. Toward the west stood the high wall of purple mountains the rocky crests of which seemed to reach the sky.

One day, when Turkey and this small boy were walking along the edge of the mesa, they heard a very queer noise coming from the north which sounded like "Sh-h-h-hiss, Sh-h-h-hiss." It seemed like the angry voice of Grey Goose whose northern home was very far away but who sometimes came to the high mesas to gather food for her brood. Turkey and First Boy looked in that direction thinking to find her close by, but no one was to be seen. Again they heard the queer sound, "Sh-h-h-hiss, Sh-h-h-hiss," but this time it came from the east. They thought it might be Sage Hen warning them away from her nest, but when they looked that way nothing was in sight. Once again the queer noise was heard and this time it came from the south. "It is a snake!" exclaimed First Boy. "We are too near its den!" They looked all around but found no snake. Then they looked far away to the north, to the east, and to the south, and in all these directions they saw moving white lines which gleamed like froth in the bright daylight. It was the foam on top of waves of deep black water that rolled high above the land. As the first wave broke with an angry hiss, another just behind it marched forward to take its place.

"What can that be?" queried First Boy.

And Turkey answered, "It is a wall of angry black water capped with white foam. But where could so much water come from?" he wanted to know. "I have seen no storm clouds in the sky."

First Boy could hardly believe his own eyes. "It has come from the lower world to drive us out of our homes," Turkey stated. "The ocean is always glad to declare war on the land!"

They listened and soon could hear plainly the rumbling, hissing voice of the advancing flood. It was a very angry voice and both Turkey and the small boy were greatly frightened. They said to each other, "We must run home quickly and tell First Man and First Woman what is happening to our land so they can call the wisemen into council and decide what is to be done." Both started to run as fast as they could but soon First Boy was far ahead of fat Turkey, who then tried to fly. He quickly found that he was too heavy and much too short of breath to make any headway through the air, so he stayed on the ground and waddled along as fast as his legs would go. First Boy arrived at the home of First Woman, gasping and so out of breath that he could hardly make her understand the message he was bringing, or the danger they were facing.

First Woman listened closely but she could not believe his story, not until she saw Turkey coming at a distance and looking so red in the face and so frightened, with his wings dragging and his feathers all rumpled, that she knew something strange and fearful must be about to happen. She had First Boy tell her again what he had seen and then, calling all her children from their play, she sent them running in every direction to warn the people in the fields and in the homes that they must prepare for danger. Many of those to whom the messages were delivered hastened to the top of some high hill to see for themselves if Turkey and First Boy had been telling the truth. When they saw the high wall of black water with its cap of hissing white foam and heard the deep angry roar of the waves beating against the land, they ran to their homes in panic. The waters of the great ocean were rolling over their land and they could do nothing to stop them.

"What shall we do? What shall we do?" they cried as they ran here and there to collect their children and to inform others of the flood. Soon all the First People who had been living so comfortably in this Fourth World knew that they must leave or be destroyed by the flood. Many wept and wrung their hands saying, "Why is the Water Monster angry with us? Why is he sending his black waters to cover our land? Where, oh where can we go? If we stay here we will all be drowned, for once that flood has covered our land it will never go away! What, oh what shall we do?"

Then they all ran to the home of First Woman to learn if she could think of a plan that might save their lives.

When the thirty-two councilmen had been called together, they agreed that all must leave the lowlands as quickly as possible, and hasten to the mountains. First Woman said, "Let everyone take as many valuable things as he can carry, not forgetting baskets or sacks of food supplies, and hurry to the highest western mountains which the waters may not cover, and where we will all be safe."

Along the western side of the Fourth World was a vast range of green mountains in the center of which stood three tall peaks with crests that were often hidden in the clouds. No one could imagine a flood so great that it could fill all the valleys and then cover the three peaks that stood so high above everything. It seemed to the First People that they would find safety on these high slopes or topmost crags.

So all the thirty-two clans of Dine'é, the Hopi, the Zuni, the Tewa, the Acoma people and many others ran to their homes to make bales and bundles, and to fill carrying baskets with their choicest possessions. The men took all they could carry strapped to their backs, while the women balanced their possessions on their heads and swung their babies in cradles across their shoulders. Everyone carried food in bags or baskets as there would be no time to gather seeds or berries along the way. It was a scattered procession for no one waited to assist his neighbor, although the members of each family did try to stay together and help the old people over the rough places.

At first the walking was not too difficult, but when they came to the foot of the mountain and started climbing its rugged slopes and rock walls, it was slow traveling. Coyote, who was in the lead, said to Badger, "Let us hurry ahead of these slow-moving people and find the best place to stay." But Badger refused to leave the others behind. He had only a small pack of food on his back, so he took time to clear the path for those who followed by digging out the sharpest stones and using his sharp teeth to clear away the brush. Hosteen Coyote had a very large bundle strapped to his shoulders, for he had brought not only a supply of food but also was carrying Water Monster's fur coat with the two babies in the pocket, as well as all the jewels he had won from the Pueblos when playing dice. He did not wish to leave any of this behind; neither did he wish to carry it all the way to the top of the mountain, so he said to Badger, "You are not making a very good path for the others to follow, why do you not let me go ahead and make the path while you cut out the brush?"

"All right," Badger grumbled sulkily, "if you can make a better path than I can, you go ahead and I will follow."

"If I must dig out all these sharp stones," Coyote stated, "you must carry my bundle as it gets in the way when I stoop over."

Badger was a strong youth with wide shoulders, and never was afraid of a little extra work, so he untied the thongs of Coyote's large bundle, lifted it from Coyote's back and transferred it to his own.

As he relinquished the bundle which held his possessions, Coyote remarked, "Be very careful of that now, as you are carrying all of our lives in that fur coat."

But Badger paid little heed as Coyote was always bragging, and answered by grumbling, "I am always careful, you need not worry about that! Let's see what sort of trail you can make."

Now Badger had small eyes and was quite nearsighted so he had not been able to select a very good path up the mountain side. On the other hand, Coyote's eyes were large and he could see for a long distance and, therefore, could pick an easy trail between the stones and bushes, so he had little work to do. Once in a while he pushed or dug a sharp stone out of the path to make it look as though he was working, and always he kept a watchful eye on Hosteen Badger and his precious load.

It was a long journey to the top of the mountain, with many detours and many steep climbs, but Coyote and Badger were among the first to arrive at a level glade just beneath the highest peak. Coyote immediately took his bundle and sorted out his carrying bag that was filled with the jewels he had won from the Pueblos, and proceeded to strap it under his arm. The two Water Babies were still asleep in the pocket of Water Monster's fur coat, and Coyote was careful to not disturb them as he threw it over his shoulders. He was sure that Water Monster had sent this flood in reprisal for the loss of his children; Coyote was sorry that he had them, but he could think of no way they could be returned.

When all the clans of First People had reached the top of the mountain, they made a great circle of green spruce boughs in which to hold their council meeting, for the air was cold there, and they needed protection from the chilly north winds that whistled around the peaks. Mountain Thunder was the ruler of the high peaks and he was not pleased to have so many people invading his domain; finally the Hopi gave him coral, the Zuni gave him white shell, and the others gave him abalone and jet, which appeased his anger. He became quite friendly and sent them warm winds and summer weather.

Among the people who had lived in the Fourth World were many who had their homes along the banks of the lakes and ponds and were as much at home in the water as on the land. These were Hosteen Otter, Hosteen Mink, Beaver, and Muskrat, along with Frog, Turtle, Snail, and Salamander and many other Water People. "We are not afraid of the flood waters," they said, "we will stay here and when the flood has gone we will live again in our own homes, while you who go away may all be killed by the evil monsters of some other land."

So the people who could swim went back to their homes; several of their friends went with them, although First Woman warned them that the water would be too deep and their homes would be destroyed. As the waters covered their land they swam around and around. When no land remained on any side and when they could not dive to the bottom they became alarmed, for they realized there was no place for them to sleep. Beaver, Muskrat, Mink, and Otter swam quickly to the mountains and, crawling out of the flood, scrambled hastily along the path the others had taken. They soon caught up with the ones who were traveling slowly and said to them, "There were many who stayed in the water, but we wish to accompany you to the mountain top." They were sad when they looked at their fur coats that had been a golden yellow, but now were the dark streaked brown of the muddy water.

It was a long time before First Woman knew what had become of the friends who had refused to come along, but one day as she was walking near the ocean she saw a seal. Looking into its face she recognized a neighbor who had lived near her in the lower world, and then she knew that these friends had been changed into Water People. She told the others about this, and that is why the Dine'é never kill or eat fish, clams, crabs or other water creatures, for fear they might be eating the flesh of descendants of their former friends and neighbors.

Turkey laden with seed-filled feathers wobbles toward the big reed in which the First People gathered to escape the flood

Chapter 4

TURKEY AND THE BIG REED

NOT ALL THE FIRST PEOPLE arrived at the top of the mountain at the same time. The eagle, hawk, cliff swallow, and some other Bird People came first, and then the locusts, dragonflies, beetles and the bees arrived. The fleetest of the Animal People came next, and after them came the slower moving creatures. The flood waters were far below, but they kept rising; every morning when First Woman looked out across the land, some familiar landmark had disappeared beneath the waves. She anxiously watched the many groups of stragglers laboring up the slopes, just barely keeping ahead of the foaming water.

33

As the days and nights passed, First Woman kept count of her people and learned that the thirty-two clans had reached the mountain top along with most of those from other tribes, and also the animal clans, the Bird People, and the creatures that were obliged to crawl. As this multitude came nearer, she could see that each traveler was carrying bundles and baskets or blankets filled with his most valuable possessions. "This is well." she said, "Wherever we go we will be able to build a world just like the one we have been obliged to leave." As she noted the different sizes and shapes of the bundles she thought, "Surely a little of everything has been saved from the flood."

It was not long before the flood waters were halfway up the mountainside and were climbing higher and higher. Everyone began asking the other, "What shall we do now? Where can we go?"

Then First Woman called the thirty-two wisemen to hold a council and learn if they had any magic or higher power that might help the people out of this danger. When all were seated inside a circle of green boughs, one man reached into his medicine bag and brought forth a large, queerly-shaped seed. "I have this seed from a bamboo tree," he said, "and if it is planted in deep soil, it will become a full-grown tree in four days."

After he had finished speaking, the next man opened his medicine bag and brought forth a similar seed. "I, too, have a bamboo seed which will grow in four days," he stated. Then each of the other wisemen held out a magic bamboo seed; in all they numbered thirty-two. A circle was marked just inside the ring of juniper branches, and thirty-two deep holes were dug an even distance apart, each to hold one of the bamboo seeds. Then the medicine men gathered in the ceremonial lodge to chant the prayers of planting and of quick growth. For four days and four nights no pause in the chanting occurred, and the seeds sent strong roots into the ground, and strong sprouts upward. The growing bamboo added four joints every night and another four joints every day. By the morning of the fifth day the thirty-two stems had increased in size until they had come together, making one huge, hollow tree thirty-two joints high and with a small peaked room at the very top.

A doorway was cut through the eastern side and thirty-two panes of rock crystal were set into the walls to provide light for the interior. Hosteen Beaver had brought a bundle of stout poles from his home in the marsh, and those oak poles were used to build ladders which led upward from room to room. As soon as that was finished, the people started marching through the doorway to find places for themselves and their belongings inside the tree. First Woman and First Man stood just inside the door where they could count all who entered.

Now when the children of First Woman had carried warnings of the flood to all the villages, the First People had hurriedly searched through their houses to gather up the things they wished to take with them to the mountain top. They made bundles of clothing and blankets to carry on their shoulders, and they filled their carrying baskets with bread and dried meat. To these baskets straps were attached so that they went across the forehead and helped support the load on the back. A few carried pottery jars filled with cactus syrup or wild honey, spruce berries and wild currants.

While all this was taking place Hosteen Turkey had arrived, puffing and panting, at the home of First Woman and her family to tell her his version of the danger that was approaching. He found a great many people hurrying here and there trying to select valuable articles, and no one would pause to listen to him. This was just as well, for Turkey's face was very red and he was so out of breath that when he tried to speak the only sound he could make was a sort of choking noise that sounded like "Obble, obble." As Turkey never regained his voice, that is the only sound he can make to this day.

When Hosteen Turkey saw that the First People were paying no attention to him, but were hurrying away to their own homes to gather the things they wished to carry to the top of the mountain, he, too, began looking around for something he might take. Glancing along the wall he noticed skeins of cotton and other fibers hanging on wooden pegs, but these he did not care for. Nor did he want the weaving sticks, spindles, or grinding stone. But when he chanced to peer into the dark storeroom he saw twenty large pottery jars standing, five against each wall, with their covers still sealed, and then he knew what he must take up the mountain.

These twenty jars held the seeds that First Woman had stored during harvest season and expected to plant in the spring. From one jar Hosteen Turkey took white corn, from the next he took blue corn, from another he took yellow corn, then red corn from the fourth, and variegated corn from the fifth. These were the five jars that were standing along the east side of the storeroom. Going to the south wall where five more ollas were standing, he took black beans, pinto beans, white beans, beeweed beans, and sunflower seeds. Along the west wall the jars contained squash, melon, gourd, pumpkin, and onion seeds. This was about all he could carry and he wondered if he could take any more. But when he opened the vessels of the north wall he saw that they contained the small seeds of tobacco, mustard, sage, mint, and peppergrass which were of little weight, and he tucked some of each under the soft feathers around his neck and on his breast, so that almost every feather was carrying a seed.

Hosteen Turkey hurried out of the house and looked around but no one was to be seen. Then he looked toward the mountain, and far away on its steep slope he could see, like lines of black ants, groups of people toiling toward the top. "Oh, dear! Oh, dear!" he cried, "I have been too slow and I will never get there in time! Is there no one to help me?"

"I will help you," sighed the wind as he changed direction in order to push Turkey from behind.

"We will help you," cried the bushes as they bent away from Turkey's path.

"I will help you," declared the earth as she rolled away the large stones and smoothed a trail for him to follow. Then Turkey ran along as fast as he could, but he did not dare to fly for fear of losing all the seeds he was carrying under his wings and under his breast feathers.

Far behind him he could hear the splash and gurgle of the great flood as it came nearer and nearer. "Perhaps it was not wise to try to take so many seeds to the top of the high mountain," he thought. "Perhaps I should drop some of them so I can run faster." But as he named the seeds to himself, he could not decide which ones to drop. So he tightened his feathers over all of them and tried to run a little faster up the steep trail, although he was now gasping for breath and his wings were almost dragging.

While all the First People were entering the tree, First Woman counted and named each one to make sure that everyone had arrived and was safely inside before the door was closed. The Bird People, who did not wish to go inside, flew up to perch on the ridges that protruded at every joint and bound the great tree together. Many earth creatures and crawling things climbed up the smooth bark to find a crevice far above, while moths and brilliant butterflies clustered at the very top, along with the small birds.

When it seemed that all were safely inside, Wind Man rattled the door and started to blow it shut, but First Woman was looking down the mountainside and said, "Wait a minute! Do not close it yet! I think I see someone coming up the mountain and it may be Turkey, for he is always the last one to make his appearance." Then Wind Man held his breath and the door stayed open so all the people could look out and see Hosteen Turkey hobbling toward them as though he were lame and very tired.

"Hurry! Hurry!" they all cried. And when he did not move any faster, they screamed, "Run, run!" But Turkey's wings and tail seemed to be dragging and he could not run any faster, even with the flood waters and the foam so near that he was spattered with the spray and deafened by the roar. When he was finally near the door, First Boy reached out and, grabbing him by the head, gave a hard pull that hauled him inside the tree. He was just in time, as the black water had reached the top of the mountain and the white line of foam swished across the tip of Turkey's dragging tail, marking it with white marks of the foam on the ends of the tail feathers. Now that Turkey was safely inside the tree, Wind Man slammed the door shut; he tied the leather thongs so they could swell when they become wet, letting not a drop of water leak through. The angry, black waters swirled and raged around the outside but they could not harm the great tree or the many people who were gathered inside.

First Woman looked around and was happy to see that all the clans and most of her friends and neighbors were there. She had counted them when they came in, and now she called each by name and asked him to tell what he had brought in his bundle that would be of use to all when they reached the new land that would be their home.

Big black Bear was the first to open his basket which was filled with acorns, hazelnuts, piñon nuts, and groundnuts. Spider Woman had a large ball of strong silk thread with which to braid rope or weave blankets. Hosteen Owl had brought several varieties of medicinal herbs and four kinds of tobacco, while grey Packrat had cactus and yucca fruit in his bundle. Porcupine was carrying many sharp needles and a ball of pitch from the piñon trees. Canary, Lark, and Oriole had gathered seeds and pollen from all the wild flowers, while Duck had brought the tubers of water plants.

Gopher had four lumps of pottery clay of different colors. Little Ant was carrying grass seeds. Bluebird Woman wore a necklace of turquoise, Mountain Jay wore one white shell and jet, and Mourning Dove had red dye and leather to make red moccasins. First Man carried his sharp stone knife and his medicine bundle. First Woman had her tow cards, weaving sticks and spindle. It seems that everyone had brought something that would be useful when they found a new world that was not covered by angry water.

Now when all these people had brought forth the contents of their baskets, jars, or bundles and put them where all could see, First Woman looked at Turkey to see what his contribution would be. She saw no basket or pottery jar, no sack or blanket-wrapped bundle of any kind, and it did not appear that he had brought a thing. This made First Woman so angry that she said to him, "Perhaps you think it is enough that you bring nothing but the feathers on your back when everyone else brings something that will be of use in the new world! You are fat and lazy and you kept all of us waiting until the angry waters almost caught you and us too! You are all speckled with the muddy water, and just look at that dirty foam on your tail feathers! Or, perhaps I am wrong and you are carrying a large bundle of precious things that we cannot see?" For she was sure that Hosteen Turkey had brought nothing at all.

Hosteen Turkey grew very red in the face when he heard First Woman say this, but he did not answer in words. First he stretched out his wings and flapped them up and down, up and down. Out fell all kinds of corn—white corn, red corn, blue corn, yellow corn, and variegated corn; then he spread the feathers of his long tail and out fell all kinds of beans and sunflower seeds. When he shook the feathers on his back and legs, out fell the seeds of squash, melon, gourd, onion, and pumpkin which made a pile on the floor. Lastly he stretched out his head and ruffled the feathers on his neck so a shower of small seeds flew in every direction—seeds of wild millet, wild rice, barley grass, tobacco, and cane grass, also mustard and sage. These were the last of the seeds, and Turkey folded his wings over his back and walked away.

During the time Turkey had been shaking his feathers the First People had watched in astonished silence, trying to count the seeds that fell to the floor. No one could think how it happened that everyone else had forgotten the precious seeds sealed in the big jars in the storeroom. If these had been left behind no farms or fields would have been planted in the new world, and no harvests in the autumn would have occurred. With no storage of food supplies, there would have been hunger and starvation during the winter. It was dreadful to think what would have happened. First Woman was very sorry now that she had called Turkey "fat and lazy" and had accused him of not bringing anything useful from the land below. As she and her helpers gathered the seeds into baskets, she spoke in a very soft voice, "I am sorry that I called Turkey 'lazy,' for he has brought us the very best things of all. When we reap our harvests we shall thank him for providing the seeds for our farms so we may have food for the winter months. From now on we shall call Turkey the 'Farm Bird,' and his feathers will be used on our prayer wands, while his beard—because it is dotted with water from the flood—will be a charm with which to bring the rain. He shall be called a 'rain maker' because of the marks of foam on his tail."

All the First People willingly agreed with First Woman and they said to each other, "From now on, Turkey shall be a very important person in our community for we will use his feathers in all our important ceremonies." Then they called Turkey and decorated him with the colors of all the seeds he had brought from the lower world. They marked his breast feathers with the colors of the corn and the brown of the tobacco seeds; they put melon seeds on his feet and hung a bean vine on his forehead. They marked his soft feathers with sunflower pollen and his beak with wild barley, while the scales on his legs were the seeds of squash and gourds. When all this decorating was finished to the satisfaction of all the First People, they told each other, "Now whenever anyone looks at Hosteen Turkey, he will be reminded of the seeds Turkey saved from the flood, and of his importance in the community. He will always be permitted to live near the homes of the First People, and no one shall do him harm."

Hosteen Locust shoots magic arrows and wins an island; Spider Woman spins a ladder on which the First People reach it

Chapter 5

THROUGH THE SKY: LOCUST WINS THIS EARTH

WHILE SO MUCH HAD BEEN taking place inside the tree, the flood waters had been rising and rising. Soon the people noticed how dark it had become, and First Woman said, "The water has risen above our crystal windows so we must all climb to a higher room." They gathered up their possessions and went up the ladder; they did not pause long in the next room as that also soon became darkened. Room after room was left behind as they climbed the ladders inside the great tree. When they reached the twelfth room, the tree began to sway and it seemed that it would tip to the east.

"I can do something about this," said east Wind, and he blew a large black cloud to brace the tree. When it started to tip toward the south, south Wind said, "I can do something about that," and he blew a large blue cloud to that side. Then west Wind blew a yellow cloud to the west and north Wind brought a white cloud from the north. Now the tree could not tip over but it shook and shivered until the birds, the moths and other flying insects had difficulty clinging to their perches on the joint ridges.

Hosteen Eagle was on the upper ridge of the tree and First Woman called to ask if he could do something to stop this dizzy motion. But she was inside the tree and he could not hear her words above the noise of the hissing water, so he took the longest feather from the middle of his tail and inserted the quill end into the very tip of the tree, making a hole through which he could listen. Again First Woman asked him to quiet the motion of the tree, so he took two feathers from each side of his tail and inserted the sharp ends into the top of the tree just below the first feather.

43

Now the tree had a crown of five feathers that grew longer and longer, but even these did not quite reach the sky; although the shaking was not stopped they did make a higher place for all the insects and the little flying creatures to perch.

As the flood rose to the twenty-fourth joint, First Woman said to First Man, "We must find an opening through the sky and make our way to the other side as this tree will soon be under water."

He thought about this for a moment and then said, "There is no opening through the hard blue dome, so we must send someone who is strong and has sharp claws to make a hole through which we may travel." They looked around and when they saw yellow Hawk sitting near Eagle on the top of the tree they asked him to fly up to the sky and see what he could do about scratching or pecking a hole through to the other side.

Yellow Hawk said he would try, so he flew to the blue dome and circled round and round underneath four times, and then started to scratch with his talons and to peck with his beak. When he grew weary, he flew back to the tree and said to First Woman, "I have made a thin place in the sky and a small crack from east to west through which I can see a little light. But I did not reach the other side."

Then First Woman sent blue Heron up to see what he could do. He, too, flew round and round under the dome four times before starting to work with his talons and his beak, but it was such hard work that he soon grew tired and returned to the tree. He told the people, "The sky is now so thin in one place that I can see the light shining through. I worked at the crack made by yellow Hawk, and I made another running north and south."

First Woman now sent big Buzzard to take his turn trying to make an opening through the sky, as she knew his beak and claws were very strong. He, too, flew up to the dome to peck and scratch at the brittle sky. On his return he reported breaking a tiny opening where the two cracks crossed in the center of the sky, but he could make it no larger and it was too small for him to pass through. First Woman looked around to find someone who would be able to crawl through this tiny opening.

As she peered through the hole made by the quills of the eagle feathers, she saw Locust standing on the tip of one feather. "He is just the one," she said. "He is small but he is strong and swift." So she asked First Man for a flint arrow point from his medicine bag and gave it to little Locust. When this arrow point was fastened securely to the top of Locust's head, he left his perch on the eagle feather and flew to the sky. The arrow point was sharp and had magic strength so the passageway was opened twice as large as it had been, but it still was not large enough to fly through. So Hosteen Locust folded his wings and started crawling through the opening that Buzzard had begun, and he had enlarged. At first the sides of the passage were hard and blue, but on top of that was nothing but black mud. When Locust reached the top of this, he looked in every direction and decided that he was on a small island of very muddy land which did not look at all like a pleasant place to live. All along the edges of this island were tall reeds, cane grass, bulrushes and willows, under which the water grass, cress and lilies were growing, and over which several varieties of birds were flying. A large white crane was in the east, a blue heron in the south, a yellow grebe in the west, and a black-and-white loon in the north. As they came near to Locust, Crane said, "What queer creature is this that has crawled up through the mud to visit our island?"

And Heron said, "It must come from the lower world, as we have had nothing like it here before."

And Grebe remarked, "It has wings and it can fly but it is not a bird because it has no feathers."

Then Loon laughed and said, "It is neither bird, fish nor animal, but it must have great magic to make a hole through the mud."

"Let us test his magic power," suggested Crane as he tossed a ball of black cloud above little Locust.

Just as it came over the center of the island, Locust shot his arrow point upward into the cloud, and immediately a heavy shower of black rain and hail filled the air. When this had cleared away, Blue Heron threw a cloud of blue mist across the island. Again Locust hit it with his arrow so lightning flickered and blue summer rain came from the sky.

"This is indeed a magic person!" Grebe exclaimed. "Let us see what he can do with a ball of yellow cloud." So saying, Grebe tossed a ball of yellow cloud across the sky, and Locust quickly shot it with his flint arrow point. Sheet lightning flashed and thunder shook the air, then the yellow rain of autumn poured down in torrents.

Now it was Loon's turn to test Locust's magic, and he threw a large ball of white cloud over the island, and, as it passed overhead, Locust took careful aim and hit it squarely in the center. Ice and snow flew in all directions, filling the air and covering the island with a blanket of white.

When this had melted away, the birds spoke to Hosteen Locust saying, "You have won the right to live on this island for your magic has proven more powerful than ours. We have to condense storm clouds into small balls to carry with us wherever we go, but we have no power to release this moisture and bring rains to the land below. Hereafter, when your voice is heard people will say, 'Listen! Locust is calling for rain.' " Then the four birds flew away, each in a different direction, leaving Locust in possession of the island.

When they had gone, Locust crawled back down through the sky passage and flew to the tree. The birds and insects crowded around asking, "Did you get through? What did you find there?"

But Locust paid no attention to them as his message was

for First Woman. He leaned over the opening in the tree's top so the people in the tree could see that he had returned. First Woman spoke to him angrily. "You were gone a long time," she scolded, "what did you find that kept you so long?"

"I had to make a larger sky hole," replied Locust, "and then I had to make a tunnel through the mud; that took a long time." Then he told her about coming out on the island and meeting the four birds who finally gave him the island. He finished by saying, "It is not a large island and the land is nothing but mud surrounded by water plants and a great lake. It will never serve as a dwelling place for all of the people."

She did not answer immediately but finally said, "Even though there is nothing but mud, I think we can make something out of it if everyone here is willing to help." She looked closely at little Locust. "What has happened to your face?" she asked. "It looks so sharp in front and flat on the sides."

Locust turned his face from side to side. "That happened before I made the sky hole large enough to crawl through," he said. "I pushed my head through the opening to look upward, but when I tried to pull it back again, the sharp edges sliced off both my round cheeks." And that is the reason why locusts, even to this very day, have sharp, thin faces.

Now it seemed that someone stronger must go to the sky and enlarge the opening, for the birds and the insects who could fly had done their best and still the passage was too small. The feather quills did not reach the blue dome, and there seemed no way for the others to reach the opening. Then First Woman said, "We need a rope! Who has a good strong rope we can use to climb to the sky?"

Mrs. Spider, who had been hiding in a dark crevice, answered, "If I were up at the opening I could spin a good strong rope from there down to the tree, but I have no wings and no way to climb upward."

"Perhaps one of the birds would carry you," suggested First Woman.

"A bird could not do it," replied Spider, "for the one that goes must fasten himself tightly to the sky in order to hold one end of the rope when I start downward toward the tree. We must find someone to carry me, someone who will stay and hold fast to one end of the rope."

Now golden Dragonfly had been sitting on the very tip of the tallest eagle feather and had heard every word that had been said. He had been one of the messengers First Woman had sent to search for an opening in the sky, and he had been the one who had brought word that the world was now entirely covered by water. Flying down to sit near the opening in the top of the tree, he said to First Woman, "Send Mrs. Spider out through this opening and I will take her to the sky." He stretched out his long shining wings to test their strength. "Then I will fasten myself to the sky near the mouth of the passage where I can hold one end of her rope."

As soon as Spider was seated between Dragonfly's wings he left the tree and flew to the sky. Grasping the edge of the opening with his claws, he curled his long, slim body underneath him until his tail was held firmly between his chest and the hard surface of the sky. His body now formed a loop to which Spider could safely fasten her rope. Then golden Dragonfly sent his spirit away to the Land of Beauty and left his body fastened firmly against the sky. To this day, you can look at the night sky and see Dragonfly, patterned in a dozen little twinkling stars, evidence of how faithfully he performed his mission.

Spider Woman worked quickly, for her friends were calling to her to make haste or they would all be drowned. She spun a thread down to the tree top where First Woman tied it inside the opening; then she went back and forth and up and down this thread twelve times, until it grew into a strong rope that would carry a heavy weight. Then quite near it, she made another just like it and spun rungs between the two until at last a strong rope ladder reached from the tree to the opening in the sky. When it was finished First Woman said to Spider, "This is a very helpful thing you have done for all the people in the tree. From now on you shall have a sheltered place in which to live, and will teach all who wish to learn how to spin strong threads and how to weave good rope and fine blankets, and you shall be known as 'The Spinner.' "

First Woman wondered who would be first to climb the ladder and enter the upper world, so she asked, "Is there anyone here who brought good, dry soil, or earth, from our home land?"

The ants answered, "We brought good soil and we brought the grass seeds to plant in it."

"Then you must be first to climb the ladder," First Woman directed, "but as you go through the passage you must each bite off bits of the hard, blue stone of the sky and take them with you; then the tunnel will be larger and also there will be some hard rock in the new world." The five clans of Ant People picked up their bundles of earth and seeds, tied them across their backs, and climbed the ladder.

When they came to the sky tunnel, they bit off chunks of hard, blue rock and carried them to the surface of the muddy island, and where they placed it we can still find beautiful blue turquoise. When they were all standing on the island, the black ant said, "I will go to the east with my seeds and soil."

The brown ant said, "I will go to the south to plant my seeds."

Yellow ant said, "I will go to the west."

And the striped ant said, "I will go to the north."

So the four ants started walking in the four directions, scattering the soil and the seeds they were carrying as they went, until all of the mud was soon covered with dry earth from which tiny blades of grass began to sprout. Then the red

49

ant said, "I will stay here and build a high piece of land with the soil I am carrying, and I will plant it with seeds of the curly grass." So he walked round and round and round until he had built a high mesa with the passage to the lower world in its exact center. Around the base and on the sides of this mesa he scattered the little pieces of colored stones he had broken from the edges of the sky opening, and to this day you will find tiny pieces of brightly colored stones on any ant hill.

The sky opening remained in the same place, but the mesa became a flat-topped mountain with other mountains all round it.

After the Ant People had disappeared through the sky to spread the dry earth and to plant the tiny grass seeds, the other small Earth People who could not fly crawled up the ladder and entered the new world. Each one carried his own load of goods and his own bit of magic with which to make this land a better place in which to live. First Woman said, "The passage is still narrow and will need widening, who will be the next to go and enlarge the tunnel?"

After a moment a thin reedy voice from a dark corner shrilled, "I am an earth dweller and am accustomed to digging in the earth. I will go next." Then Dung Beetle stepped forth with a ball of humus on his back.

"We will go with him," announced the striped beetle and the yellow beetle who were carrying their loads of humus under their wings. Then a big stag beetle appeared with his load on his horns saying, "Our jaws are strong and we all make tunnels through the earth, so we will see what we can do."

"So will we," said the grasshoppers who had been clinging to the feather quills. "We, too, live in the soil." Then they started to climb the ladder, one after the other; the grasshopper chief, who was old and grey, went last.

Now when Turkey saw the beetles and the grasshoppers climbing toward the sky he became very angry and shouted, "Who are these people who are going up to the new world?

Where did they come from, and who said they could go? I did not see them anywhere, and they are carrying nothing that will be of any use to anyone. If they live near our corn-fields they will destroy the young plants so we will have no harvests."

First Woman answered Turkey, saying, "They are carrying pollen under their shells and if they do not go our corn will have no kernels on the cobs. And beside that, they carry in their cheeks a brown medicine which cures insanity." Then she added, "Grasshopper Maiden will tell us when the corn is ripe and will teach us the harvest songs."

Turkey was not at all happy as he watched the beetles and grasshoppers disappear through the tunnel, and muttered to himself, "They will ruin our corn and if I see any in our fields I will destroy them." Even today, Turkey destroys all the grasshoppers he can find.

First Woman looked at the sky opening and said, "Many have gone through but it is still a small tunnel. Who will try to make it larger?"

"I will try," offered the blind mole as he started up the ladder. He gnawed at the hard edge of the sky and then disappeared in the passage. He dug through the mud, but when he came to the dry earth he lost his direction and dug his tunnel round and round so no one ever did know where he came to the surface. Gopher and Chipmunk went next but they became lost in the maze of tunnels the mole had made and failed to appear. Little Prairie Dog followed them and thought the tunnel was large enough, so he did no digging at all.

Now First Woman was becoming worried as the water was almost as high as the tree so she looked around to find someone larger, who had strong teeth and claws. She asked the waiting people, "Which one of you can work very fast and will not be afraid to dig through rock, or loose earth, or mud?"

Big, fat Badger stepped in front of her and said, "I am

not afraid to dig through rock, or earth, or mud, and I am a very fast worker."

"Very well," said First Woman, "you may go next, but you must be sure to hurry!"

Just then Coyote came walking up to where the two were talking and said, "I had better go with Badger so we can dig twice as large a hole and get through twice as fast."

"Oh, no!" said First Woman, "you would only get in Badger's way and cause a delay."

But Coyote refused to listen and said, "Badger can work on one side and I will work on the other; we are friends and we always work together."

"Very well," agreed First Woman, "but make sure the tunnel is wide enough for our largest people."

Coyote was saying to himself, "If I stay here she is sure to ask me to take my turn at digging, but if I go with Badger I may not need to dig at all!"

Then the two climbed the ladder and began gnawing and scratching at the hard blue surface of the sky, breaking away chunks so the opening would be larger. Coyote knew that First Woman and the people in the tree were watching them, so he pretended to work very hard. Badger worked energetically, tossing chunks of rock in every direction, but Coyote chipped off only a few small pieces. It was not long until Badger had made a good-sized opening through which he could crawl to start work on the earth and mud on the other side. No sooner was Badger through this part of the tunnel than Coyote crawled in behind him. Badger continued to dig, throwing the loose soil backward between his hind legs to clear it out of the tunnel. As a ball of dirt came toward him, Coyote would grab it in his paws and toss it over his shoulder so it would drop out of the sky opening. It appeared to those who were watching below that Coyote was doing most of the work, as most of the soil came from his side of the tunnel.

Before Coyote had left the tree and started to climb the ladder, he had placed Water Monster's fur coat, with the two babies asleep in the inside pocket, in a hidden crevice, but he still carried the medicine bag containing his winnings strapped over his shoulders. As he worked in the tunnel, the strap holding the bag kept slipping off his shoulder little by little and now, as he gave a harder toss than usual, it slid off and followed the dirt he was throwing through the opening and down into the water surrounding the tree. Coyote thought he saw a hand or paw reach out of the water and grasp the bag. "Oh dear!" he said to himself, "the Water Monster has recovered his jewels, but anyway I still have the Water Babies."

When Badger came to the mud he was obliged to work more slowly as it stuck to his paws, and he was forced to pat it into balls before he could toss it backward. Coyote did not like the mud, so he crawled to one side where he could catch the balls without being hit by them before tossing them out through the opening. It did not take Badger long to tunnel through the mud. When he came to the dry top soil, Coyote started working at his side to make it appear that he had been digging all the way. When they had finished, Badger sat panting near the mouth of the hole, for he was quite exhausted by his labor; Coyote sat down beside him and panted loudly also, pretending that he, too, was quite out of breath.

After resting a few moments, the two clambered down through the passage to make their reports to First Woman. Badger said, "We have made a wide tunnel through the sky so now all the First People will be able to enter the new world."

And Coyote said, "Our tunnel is straight and will lead you to the dry land of the new world, but if you follow the crooked tunnels of the blind mole you will always live in the earth."

Then Coyote and Badger went to a dark corner where they tried to clean their faces and coats of the sticky, black mud that clung to them. But the more they rubbed and brushed, the harder the dirt clung to their fur. When the

First Woman with headdress of five eagle feathers—magic feathers that
bring blessings to the wearer

First People came to thank them for their efforts, they saw that Coyote had black paws from catching the mud balls and a speckled coat from tossing the dirt over his shoulder, while Badger had black paws and forearms, a black streak on his face and black along his back, all made by the sticky, black mud. Although many tried to brush it off, they did not succeed, so Badger and Coyote bear those markings to this very day.

Coyote knew that Badger was an honest and industrious person who never tried to shirk his duty or play tricks on his companions, but he also thought him to be a dull, slow-witted chap who could be easily cheated. "I will stay near Badger," Coyote said to himself, "and when hard, disagreeable work is to be done I will trick him into doing it. And when he finds food to eat, I will beg a share." So from that day to this, Coyote and Badger live along the same hillsides and hunt in the same valleys.

As soon as Coyote and Badger had returned with word that the passage was now large enough for even the big, brown bear, the First People gathered their bundles and baskets and began leaving the tree. The eagles, hawks, buzzards, owls and other large birds went first, followed by the smaller birds, and the butterflies and moths, for these feathered folk had been waiting outside the tree. Then came the small and the medium-sized animals which quickly climbed the ladder and disappeared in the tunnel.

White Wolf and brown Bear looked at the slim ladder and refused to test its strength until Mountain Lion leaped ahead of them and clawed her way to the top. The ladder did not bend or break but it was swaying badly with the motion of the tree. After the animals had gone, the First People went by clans and families. First the Hopi, the Zuni, and the other Pueblo peoples, then the Apache and the Plains Indians. The thirty-two clans of Navaho followed, and then only First Man and First Woman were left in the tree, where the water was now up as far as the little, peaked room at the very top. First Man said to First Woman, "You climb the ladder first and I will follow."

But First Woman said, "No, you climb the ladder first, as I have some things I wish to save from the flood." So First Man tied his bow and quiver of arrows on his back, put his magic flint knife in his medicine bag and climbed the ladder. First Woman gathered her possessions into a blanket which she tied across her shoulders; then she turned and cut the bottom of the ladder loose from the tree. After she had climbed a few rungs, she pulled the lower end up and wrapped it around her waist, and as she climbed further she took the ladder with her. Just as she reached the edge of the blue sky she stooped down and, one by one, pulled the five eagle feathers from the top of the tree. These she placed on her back and then wound the spider's ladder around and around her body to hold them in place.

Many hands helped her through the opening, as she was so wrapped with rope and bundles she could hardly move. When she stood in the midst of the crowd that was waiting for her, they were all astonished at the number of things she carried. First they unwound the rope ladder, which now had grown small and as delicate as a spider's web, and stretched it on the ground where all could see. "From now on," they said, "women shall do the weaving and they shall wear woven goods instead of buckskins."

Then they took the five feathers, which had returned to normal size, and placed them in a headdress that she would wear when taking part in religious ceremonies. "These are magic feathers," they said, "and will bring blessings to the wearer." So, today, in many religious rites, and in many of the sacred sandpaintings, the female characters will be seen wearing headdresses adorned with five tall eagle feathers.

First Man and First Woman placing the Water Babies that Coyote had stolen in a small boat for their return to Water Monster

Chapter 6

THE MONSTERS AND THE GREBES

WHEN ALL THE FIRST PEOPLE had arrived in the new world and the passageway through which they had come was empty, everyone began looking around to see just what sort of place this might be. All the land they could see was flat, with the exception of a high mesa in the center, which had been built with earth brought from the lower world by the Red Ant People. The Beetle People had built other high places in the four directions, and then the land slanted to the ocean where it disappeared beneath the rolling waves. It was a discouraging sight, but it was not as bad as it had been, for the ants had planted the tiny seeds of the low grasses, and the beetles had brought seeds for the small bushes which now covered the ground with green vegetation. But there were no mountains or high hills, no rivers or creeks, no houses, fields or trees. This world would need a great deal of work before it would be a pleasant place in which to live.

The Hopi, the Zuni, and the other peoples who had been the first to arrive were not pleased with this land; they decided to travel farther east until they found something they liked better. When they came to the ocean, they called upon Rainbow to make a great arch over the water, and on this bridge they traveled to another island. Many of the animals such as the puma, the lynx, the blue fox, and the wildcat went with them, also a number of birds, namely, the buzzard, magpie, eagle and the turkey. So now only the thirty-two clans of the Dine'é were left in this place, and about half of the birds and animals that had come from the lower world.

As First Woman was considering the initial steps to be taken, Locust came flying to tell her that water was rising to the top of the tunnel which led to the lower world, and would soon be pouring out over the land; already a lake was growing larger and larger. "It must be Water Monster who is doing this!" exclaimed First Woman. "He is the only one who could command the water to rise so high. We will all be in danger until we find out what he wants!"

"Someone has something that belongs to Water Monster," declared First Man. "And I think it must be Coyote, for I have seen him slinking here and there, wearing a very queer spotted fur coat over his shoulders."

"We must look under all the fur coats and learn if there is anything that belongs to Water Monster hidden beneath," declared First Woman. Then all the fur bearing animals were lined up in front of First Man and First Woman to be searched for stolen goods. Mink and Beaver, Otter and Muskrat were searched without finding anything. Then Wolf and Porcupine, Badger and Coyote were next in line. When it was Coyote's turn, they saw the spotted coat he was wearing over his own grey fur, and First Man said, "What is this? It looks like the coat Water Monster was wearing in the lower world."

"Yes," said Coyote, "it did belong to Water Monster, but it is mine now as I won it in a game we were playing."

All the people who were listening agreed that Coyote was telling the truth, for they had watched the games and knew that Coyote had won.

"Well if it is not the coat Water Monster wants, it must be something that is hidden inside," First Man stated. "Take it off and let us see if there is something in the pockets."

Coyote took the coat off and handed it to First Woman who quickly discovered the two Water Babies. "So this is what has caused all of our trouble!" she exclaimed. "This is why we were forced to leave our pleasant homes and seek a new place to live! This is why we again are threatened with flood waters! We must return these children to Water Monster at once!"

Then First Man and First Woman walked out on a point of land that projected into the lake and, when they reached the water, First Woman folded the coat into a small boat that would carry the babies across the water. In the very center of the lake was a large blue bubble that moved in a circle, and when the coat came near it the bubble burst and sent a fountain of water high into the air. When the water settled down, the coat with the babies had disappeared and the water of the lake was receding through the opening.

Soon the lake became a round, bottomless body of water that has remained the same to this day, but the land around it which had been under water turned into deep, muddy swamps that sheltered monsters of many kinds. The cranes and the herons, the geese and the grebes brought seeds of bulrushes, cane grass, sedges and willow which soon grew thick and tall in the marsh, providing places for the wading birds to build their nests and raise their young. But this was not a safe place for the Dine'é, for here lived two of the most dangerous monsters in the new world. On one side was a great toad-like creature with spines like sharp horns along its back, while on the other side lived a long, scaly monster with double rows of sharp teeth.

For a while these monsters did not trouble the Dine'é; but once, when a small girl walked too near the rushes, a great scaly tail slapped her into the marsh; and once, when a woman was gathering reeds to weave into mats, an enormous paw reached out for her and she was never seen again. So the First People did not walk near the swamps nor did they walk along the ocean shore for here, too, was danger. In the ocean was the great Sea Serpent that caught people in its coils, and there was the black *Ch'indii* with eight long arms, and there were fish with sharp teeth, beside enormous clams that could eat a child in one bite. These ocean monsters did not come on the land to trouble the First People, but when the storms lashed the waters into great waves that rolled over the land, people and animals were washed away and never seen again.

As soon as the sea monsters and the marsh dwellers learned that people were living on the island, they hid along the banks and in the tangled sedges to catch anyone who might walk too near. So now the First People lived in constant fear, for these marsh giants and sea beasts were so large that their hunger was never satisfied, and they were always searching for more animals or more people to devour. It seemed that every family had lost some friend or relative, and everyone grew sad and disheartened. They tried to hide but there were not many places that were safe when the huge foaming waves came sweeping over the land, and there was no way of knowing how many would be swept out to sea.

"We must do something about this," First Woman decided.

"What is there to be done?" asked First Man. "We have no place to go."

"That is true," First Woman answered, "but we can place guards on every side of the land who will keep watch and let us know when they see the great monsters coming from the marshes or when the Sea Serpent is lashing the ocean into high waves. Then we can go to the high places where we will be safe from harm."

"This is a very good idea," agreed all the First People. "We will appoint four guards that can fly, so we will not be afraid of the high waves or of the beasts from the swamps. Let us station one guard on each side of the land and then we will always have warning when danger threatens."

First Woman looked around at all the Bird People who made their homes near the water. She looked at small Duck, but he was not tall enough to keep watch above the reeds; then she looked at Loon, but he, too, had very short legs; and it was the same with grey Goose. On the other side she saw Heron, Crane, Bittern, and Grebe, all of whom stood on long stilt-like legs which raised their heads above the reeds and marsh grasses. Bittern's legs were not long, but he had a long neck that served to make him tall.

"Some of these must act as guards," First Woman stated, but she did not know which to choose.

Finally First Man said, "Let us hear how they would give the alarm, and then we can decide."

So Heron stepped forth and gave a thin, reedy cry and all the people shook their heads.

Then Crane flapped his long wings and drummed, "Boom, boom, boom," and the people nodded as this sound could be heard a long distance.

Now it was Bittern's turn and he pointed his long sharp bill straight at the sky as he squawked, "Quark! Quark!" He sounded so queer that the people laughed, and he went to hide in the reeds.

Grebe had a long, slim body and a narrow bill, and when he stepped forth to give his call it proved to be a high shrill whistle that cut the air like a knife. Everyone agreed that this could be heard at the greatest distance.

First Woman called the four tallest grebes and stationed a grey one near the shore of the ocean on the north to report when high waves were threatening from that direction. A blue grebe was stationed in the south and given the same instructions. Then a yellow grebe was placed near the marsh in the east and told to watch for the toad-like beast with wide jaws; and a speckled grebe was given a place near the marsh in the west and told to watch for the scaly monster with many teeth. Now the First People could move about from place to place, but they were always listening for the shrill whistle given by one of the guards, and they did not think it wise to venture far from the safety of their highest land.

For a time the water monsters and the marsh beasts who lurked near the shores of the ocean or the borders of the swamp found no animals or people to satisfy their hunger, as the grebes whistled shrill warnings telling of their where-abouts, and no one ventured near. Finally the two who lived in the marshes grew bolder and waddled out across the dry land, going at first just a little way from their lairs, and then further and further as they still failed to find food. The yel-low grebe and the speckled grebe gave their warnings over and over, but they knew it would not be long until the great toad and the scaly monster would try to follow the people to their refuge on the higher mesa.

"We must not allow this to happen!" cried yellow grebe. "We must think of some plan to save the First People from these monsters."

"But what can we do?" asked speckled grebe. "They are a hundred times our size and the very strongest creatures in the world!"

"The strongest are not always the smartest," stated the yellow grebe. "We must use our wits to work out some plan for destroying these beasts before they can harm the First People."

For a time the two grebes talked of snares of vines, such as were sometimes used to catch birds, but no vines growing in the marshes or elsewhere were strong enough to hold such enormous animals. Then they thought of digging pits for traps. But who could dig a pit so deep that these two could not climb out? However, it was certain that they must think of some plan at once, for the monster toad was waddling slowly toward them from the east, peering first one way and then the other with his tiny near-sighted eyes; while a scaly monster could be seen in the west, sometimes standing on his powerful hind legs, and sometimes walking on all fours, swinging his head from one side to the other.

Suddenly the yellow grebe and the speckled grebe knew what they would do. The yellow bird flew to a place just in front of the great toad and began limping and flapping his wings to attract attention, while the speckled grebe acted the same way in front of the scaly beast. Now the yellow grebe was carrying a rattle made of small sea shells tied together with strings of sea vine, which made a soft tinkling sound when it was shaken. And the speckled grebe was carrying a rattle made of slim pieces of rock crystal tied with fibers from a grape vine; this made a sweet, ringing noise. As the two monsters came toward the two birds, they began shaking their rattles and walking toward each other. Now one of the monsters had round, protruding eyes, while the other had narrow slits for eyes which were almost hidden by the heavy lids, so neither could see very far ahead of its nose, but both were very keen of hearing. The two birds stayed just close enough to them so they could see that something was moving in front of them. Then the birds made all the noise they could with their rattles so the beasts would follow the sound.

Faster and faster walked the grebes! Faster and faster came the monsters! Finally they were all running as fast as they could, only the birds were careful not to leave their pursuers too far behind. Sometimes they would pause until it seemed as though the beasts could reach out and grab them, then they would move ahead rapidly to set a fast pace for the monsters, who thought they were a couple of Dine'é who could not fly. At other times when the marsh beasts had chased birds, they had run a little way and then taken to the air so they were soon out of danger. But these two did not seem to know how to fly and the beasts were sure they would soon be caught.

The two grebes were quite out of breath when they met in the middle of the peninsula, and the yellow grebe said, "Now!" and the speckled grebe said, "Now!" Then both stretched out their long wings and flew straight up into the air. The two great monsters who were just behind them, running as fast as they could, came together with a thud that shook the whole land and caused the First People to hide in their safest places.

"What is this?" exclaimed the great toad as he backed away from the scaly monster. "You have no right to be hunting on my part of the land!"

"I am not hunting on your land," answered the scaly one. "This is my hunting ground and I would like to know what right you have to be here!"

So they argued back and forth until both were too angry to say anything more, and then a fight began. They bit and stomped and rolled over and over; they squealed and bellowed and moaned while the blood splattered all over the land so all the rocks turned red, and they have remained red to this very day. Finally, when they were both too weak to fight any more, they crawled slowly back to their marshy lairs to die. The fish and the frogs ate the meat from their bones, which sank into the mud and gradually turned to stone. Hundreds of years later, men with picks and shovels came to uncover these fossils and take them to museums where the people who come to see them are amazed at their age and size.

Now when the First People heard that the monsters from the marshes were dead and would trouble them no more they were very glad and called the yellow grebe and the speckled grebe to a meeting.

"This is a wonderful thing you have done for us," they told the two. "From now on you shall be rulers over all the marsh and swamp lands, both in the west and in the east, and no one will disturb your nests or seek to drive you away." And all Navaho heed this decision, even at the present time.

Small Duck carrying First Man's medicine bag on a mission to get four
colored stones from the ocean depths

Chapter 7

SMALL DUCK AND THE MOUNTAINS

ALL THE PEOPLE OF THE NEW
world were glad that the swamp beasts were dead, for now
the wading birds and the smaller water animals could build
their homes among the reeds and willows without fear of
harm from these enemies.

"Now there will be more land on which we can live!"
exclaimed First Woman. But even as she was speaking they
all heard the long shrill whistle of the grey grebe that was
watching the ocean shore at the north; immediately following this they heard a similar warning from the south. From
the sound they knew that great walls of angry water were
rolling toward them from those two directions, and were
being lashed into waves by the mighty sea serpents who lived
in the ocean caves.

"Why did we come to this land?" the First People were asking each other. Then they said, "We are still in danger of being drowned!"

After this was said, several people started voicing complaints. "There is nothing here for us to live on except the plants and food we brought with us, and when that is gone we will starve!"

"How many have been swept away by the ocean waves?" asked a third.

"Several of our children and nearly all of our Old Ones who could not run fast," was the reply.

So they all looked sad and discouraged as they gathered their belongings to make a hasty trip to a high mesa around the central lake. There the Ant People had built the land so high that the waves could not reach them.

"Is there any way in which we can destroy the water monsters?" First Woman wanted to know.

"Destroying one or two would do no good," replied First Man. "The ocean is so vast that it shelters many monsters of many kinds."

First Woman considered this and then said, "We should have a high wall all around the borders of this land so we can live safely without fear of being carried into the ocean by the angry waves."

All the First People agreed to this and nodding their heads said to each other, "Yes! Yes! That is right. We need mountains such as we had in the lower world to stand between us and the dark water."

Now the ants, the earthworms, the gophers, and the prairie dogs that had built comfortable homes underground were the earth movers. As soon as it was decided that walls must be built on all four sides of the land, First Woman asked the Ant People to build the wall at the east, the gophers were requested to do the same in the south, earthworms were to go to work in the west and prairie dogs in the north. So these Earth People went to the four sides of the land and started to build earthen dams along the shores. Bit by bit they placed the soil in ridges, but when old Ocean saw what was taking place he gave a mighty roar and sent his waves smashing across the land so the ridges were washed away and the beach along the ocean was low as ever.

When the people saw how easily these dunes had been washed away, they all said to each other, "We must have rock to build our mountains, as earthen hills are of no use."

"Did anyone bring rock or even small stones from the lower world?" First Man asked. No one answered. His question started the people to thinking.

"Where can we find the rock we need?" they all wondered.

None was in the center of the land, nor as far as they could see. Then First Woman sent Locust to fly around the edge of the land to find any stones the great waves had washed onto the shore. Locust made the journey quickly and returned with the report that there were no stones. Now the First People became quite discouraged and began thinking of the high mountains, the peaked rocks, and the pleasant hills of the country in which they had lived before coming to this flat land. They knew they could not go back because those places were now all under the ocean, but oh, how they wished this new country was not so flat! If only there were something they could do about it!

Now First Man, who really possessed a great deal of magic power which he used only on occasions of dire necessity, being fearful of diminishing its strength, pondered a long time and then said, "Who among you is considered very brave? I have a plan whereby we will be able to build a wall of mountains all around this land, but I need a very brave person to help. Who is willing to do a very dangerous thing to help me carry out this plan?" And he looked around at all the Dine'é, at the animals, the birds, and all who were standing in the circle.

"I am brave!" screamed Eagle as he stood with folded wings and flashing eyes not far from First Man. "I can fly among the clouds when the deep thunder rolls and the lightning flashes! I can fly straight toward the face of the sun! I fear nothing!"

"I am brave," growled big Bear as he lifted his shaggy head above all who were standing near. "Look how big and strong I am, and how I can enter the darkest caves with no fear of the lion or the wolf who might be hiding there!"

"I am brave!" sang fat Bumblebee as he flew above First Man's head. "Everyone knows that I carry a poison arrow, and they all step from my path when they hear my war chant." Then he buzzed his wings until they looked like silver spray, to show how fast he could fly.

"Very well!" said First Man as he looked from one to the other, considering the three who claimed to be brave. "I am glad three brave people are here, for if the first one fails in this mission, the next will surely succeed." He was silent a moment and then continued, "Are you willing to go down to the mountains, that are now at the bottom of the dark waters, to find stones of four colors to bring to me? On the east mountain lies a stone of clear white crystal, on the south mountain is a stone of blue turquoise; at the west will be found a stone of yellow jasper, and at the north lies a stone of black jet. Someone must bring me those four stones; I need them to form the hearts of the four mountains."

When he had finished speaking, a great silence fell upon the people who were looking hard at the three who had declared their bravery: big Bear, fat Bumblebee, and grey Eagle.

Then Eagle spoke in a low, shamed voice saying, "I cannot do that. I would lose my breath in the dark water, and if my feathers became wet and heavy I would never be able to fly back to land." Spreading his great, grey wings he flew far away into the sky. Now all the people turned to look at big Bear who had said that he was not afraid of anything.

Bear stood first on one foot and then on the other while he hung his head and examined his paws, so as not to look

Small Duck volunteering to go into the ocean's dark waters to get rocks
and earth for the First Peoples' mountains

at the waiting people. "I cannot do that!" he grumbled. "I
am not as strong as the black Sea Monster, and I cannot see
under water, so I could not find the four stones." Then big
Bear shuffled away to hide in his dark cave where the people
would not see him.

"I cannot do that!" whispered fat Bumblebee as he
lighted on a low bush and buzzed his wings very fast, trying
not to seem ashamed. "The dark water would not be good for

my wings or for my beautiful velvet coat, and I cannot swim at all." Then he flew away to his home.

First Man and all the First People were very sad and disappointed when these three had gone, for it seemed that no one would carry out his plan. Everyone was afraid to go down into the dark water to find the four colored stones he needed to make this new world a safe place in which to live. No words were spoken, but everyone was thinking that someone else should be brave enough to go. Beaver looked at Turtle, and Otter looked at Frog, each one thinking that the other was a good swimmer and should offer to make the trip.

Then suddenly they all heard a small, soft voice that said, "I am not brave! I am very much a coward in my heart! I cannot fly high in the face of the sun, nor can I walk into the deep cave where a lion might be hidden. No people step from my path when they meet me, for I carry no poison arrow and I sing no war chant, but if no one else will go to the bottom of the deep water for the four colored stones, at least I can try." Then small Duck stepped forward and stood in front of First Man and First Woman.

Now when the First People saw that it was small Duck who had spoken these brave words, they acted very surprised and were extremely rude. They shook their heads and laughed and nudged each other. "Look," they said to each other, "what a great thing it is that small Duck thinks he can do!" And someone remarked, "As soon as he is in the deep water, the black Monster or Sea Serpent or Scaly Fish will swallow him like a ripe thimbleberry. Besides, how could such a small person bring four heavy stones from the bottom of deep dark water?"

But First Man walked over to small Duck and said, "Very well! You can try! No one could do more than that!" Then he took off his beaded medicine bag and slipped the strap over small Duck's head so the bag hung down on the soft feathers of his breast. "Take this with you," he commanded, "and when you find the stones of four colors, slip them quickly into this bag where they will be safe. Whatever is placed in this medicine bag belongs to me, and no one will dare to touch it or take it from you."

When he had finished speaking, he sprinkled small Duck from head to foot with sacred pollen taken from the great bulrushes that grew at the edge of the lake. This he did so small Duck need fear no harm from the deep dark water. But First Man had no magic words or powerful medicine to give small Duck to use against the slimy Sea Serpent, Scaly Fish, or the black Water Monster.

The First People stood around watching these preparations and feeling very sorry for small Duck. They knew now that he really was going to dive into the deepest part of the ocean and try to find the four colored stones which First Man needed to build his mountain wall. They said, one to another, "He is much too small! His wings are not wide enough and he cannot stay under water long enough! See how the medicine bag hangs down in front of him! It will slow his progress so the monsters will overtake him! He cannot swim fast with that on his neck! I fear we will never see small Duck again."

Small Duck paid no attention to these remarks, but they did little to bolster his courage, and his heart beat fast with fear as he walked toward the water. At the water's edge he spread out his swift, smooth wings and widened his long beautiful tail of which he was very proud. No other water bird boasted a tail as long and graceful as that of small Duck. He looked around quickly to see if his friends were watching and then, with a couple of hops, he soared into the air and flew far away over the dark water. He flew and he flew until he had left the land out of sight behind him and, finally, he came to the center of the ocean where the water was the deepest. There he folded his wings over the medicine bag, pointed his bill straight down and dropped fast. Oh, so fast! into the dark water. Down, down went small Duck like a swift arrow, and the water grew colder and colder and the light grew dimmer and dimmer.

"How can I ever know when I reach the mountains?" thought Duck. But suddenly the medicine bag, which had led the way, hit something solid. "This is one mountain," thought small Duck. "This is where I must find one of the stones." Gazing about, he saw a white stone that shone so brightly he knew it must be one of the stones First Man wanted. Picking it up quickly, he popped it into the medicine bag. Now he must move to the south before the sea monsters knew he was here. At the southern mountain he found the blue stone; at the western mountain he picked up the yellow stone; and in the north he found a stone of shining black jet.

Now small Duck had the four stones safe in his medicine bag, and, so far, he had not been bothered by the Water People. He had come as fast as a streak of silver light and he had worked so quickly that the stones had been found before the Water People could recover from their surprise. But when he turned his bill upward and started paddling his feet to swim toward the surface of the water, he saw a long, shining serpent with open jaws coming straight toward him. Small Duck paddled this way and then he paddled that way, but all the time he did not forget to go upward as fast as he could. When he looked to the other side he saw a great scaly monster with many teeth swimming dangerously near. Again he was obliged to dodge this way and then that way to avoid being caught, while still going upward to reach the surface. Small Duck was becoming very tired now and the medicine bag, which had been of help when he was going down into the water, was so full of heavy stones that the strap rumpled the feathers and hurt his neck. He had not realized that the stones would be so heavy.

"Shall I slip this strap from my neck and drop the bag of stones into the deepest part of the dark water," thought small Duck, "or shall I open the flap and drop just one stone to make the bag a little lighter?" As he was slowing down to do this, he saw a great, brown monster moving toward him with three long arms reaching out to grab him. Quick as a flash small Duck changed his course and darted upward, forgetting all about his decision to throw away some of the stones. He remembered that First Man and all the First People would

The narrow escape of Duck from Scaly Fish

be waiting for him at the edge of the water and that they would expect him to have all four of these colored rocks. Nor could he drop the medicine bag which belonged to First Man, no matter how much it hurt his neck, for if it was gone, First Man would lose all his magic power. Bravely small Duck clung to his heavy load and paddled faster with his feet. Just when the great-fish-with-many-teeth made a grab at him, small Duck's head popped out of the water into the clear air. Then his shoulders came above water and he spread his wings with a cry of joy. But alas! At that moment Scaly Fish leaped ahead and made a grab at him, and closed his jaws with a snap right on small Duck's long, beautiful tail! For a moment the brave little duck felt himself being pulled back and back toward the dark water. "Oh! No!" he cried, "this will never

do at all!" And with a great flapping of wings he broke loose
and flew upward leaving the longest feathers of his beautiful
tail caught in the shark's cruel teeth.

It was not easy to fly with most of the feathers missing
from his tail, and he was so very tired from his swim, but he
would not give up now. Straight as an arrow he flew toward
the land where all the First People were waiting to see if he
would ever come back. Hosteen Hawk was the first to see him
from a great distance and began screaming, "Here he comes!
Here he comes! I can see him! I can see him!"

Then Falcon, whose eyesight was very keen, cried, "He is
carrying the heavy medicine bag! He has the stones! He has
the stones!"

By that time everyone could see small Duck flying toward
them over the dark water. They were all very excited and
jumped up and down crying, "He has returned from the
deep ocean! He has brought the four stones!"

Small Duck was flying slowly now as he was very weary
and the bag was fast becoming too heavy. He folded his wings
and landed in front of First Man, who was standing not far
from the water's edge. Small Duck was glad that his perilous
mission had been accomplished. He said nothing for he was
having a hard time gasping for breath. When he slipped the
strap from his neck, First Man took the bag and started to
open the flap; all the others crowded around to get a glimpse
of the contents. While this was being done and no one was
looking at him, small Duck slipped away and hid himself in
the tall reeds that grew by the water's edge, for he was quite
ashamed of his short tail. He was hoping that when the big
scaly fish opened his jaws the long, beautiful feathers from his
tail would float to the shore where he could find them. So he
stayed in the shallow water among the reeds to watch for
them, but he never found them, and to this day all ducks
have short tails.

First Man had taken the heavy medicine bag to open it
while all the First People crowded around to obtain a glimpse

of the four stones that had been brought from the mountains under the dark water. They were quite disappointed when they saw them, for they did not look any different from the stones they had used for building their houses in the lower world.

But First Man seemed satisfied and said, "Yes, these are the right ones! Now we will soon have four mountain walls to protect us from the raging ocean waves." He took out the white stone and carried it to the eastern edge of the land; he blew on it four times so that it grew higher and higher with each breath, until he ceased blowing. Going to the north of the land, he again blew four times, and the tall white rock spread in that direction until it could go no further. First Man then blew on the opposite side and the land grew in that direction, forming a long range of white mountains that completely shut out the ocean along the eastern side. First Man took the blue turquoise stone to the south and shaped a long range of blue mountains there, in the same way he had created those in the east. Then he created a range of still higher mountains in the west, and in the north he made many black peaks. Now the land was completely surrounded by high mountains, but in growing so large and wide, they had spread over the countryside so far that little space remained on which the First People might live. When First Man saw how small the level land had become, he called the four Wind People to come to his assistance. Each of the four winds blew with all its might against one of the mountain walls and, one by one, each of the mountain ranges moved slowly back into the water, leaving mesas, small hills, valleys and desert land where they had been standing. So when the winds ceased blowing, all kinds of land were present on which the First People could make their homes.

Now when all this was finished and the First People felt safe from the ocean waves and the hungry sea monsters, they began looking around to see what had become of small Duck. They wished to thank him for his bravery and to say they were sorry they had made fun of him. They searched and searched, but small Duck was nowhere to be found. He had hidden himself in the reeds and tangled grasses, as he did not want the First People to laugh at his short tail.

When they failed to locate his hiding place, First Man said to all the people, "Small Duck proved himself the bravest of all. He undertook the hard and dangerous task even when his heart was full of fear. He brought us the four stones that now stand like a great fortification between us and the dangerous waters. From now on, no one of us shall ever try to harm small Duck, or destroy his nests." And to this day, that law is carefully observed by the Navaho people.

The turquoise-masked Sun and white-masked Moon of the First People atop the highest Mountains

Chapter 8

THE SUN, MOON AND STARS

In this present, or fifth World, the First People had four lights which had been brought from the lower world. White light appeared over the eastern mountains, blue light spread across the sky from the southern mountains, yellow light came from the western peaks, and darkness from the north. These lights were far away and carried no heat, so the air was always of one temperature and no seasonal changes occurred although there was darkness and daylight.

"We do not have enough daylight," the people complained. "We surely need more light."

So First Woman sent Glowworm to the east, and told Fox Fire to go to the south, Lightning Beetle to the west, and Firefly to the north. Then, when anyone needed extra light, these four were ready to serve him.

78

For a time this plan worked very well, but it was not long before the First People were saying, "These lights are too small. They flicker on and off so they are of little use to us. We cannot work in such dim light!"

Then others asked, "How can we see to do anything? We do not have night eyes like Hosteen Owl or little Bat!"

It seemed that First Woman could never please them. Finally she thought of Fire Man and his glowing mountain, so she sent a messenger to ask the Fire Man if he could help her.

"Yes," agreed Fire Man, "I can make the land bright all around Fire Mountain, but the light will not reach the edges of the land, and there will be smoke." After that flames leaped high above the mountain top, and there was no more darkness for some distance. But soon the people were again complaining.

"We do not like the heat and the smoke that is coming from Fire Mountain," they declared. "The heat scorches the earth and we are choked by the smoke!"

As everyone was complaining and no one was satisfied, First Woman decided that she must find a different way by which to light the earth. After consulting with the council of wisemen, she told her helpers to bring her a large, flat slab of the hardest and most durable rock they could find. After visiting every mountain and rocky pinnacle, they returned with a large, flat slab of quartz; it was twice as long as it was wide, and, when the helpers had placed it on the ground in front of her, First Woman decided it was large enough to make two round wheels of equal size. She had hoped to make four in order to have one for each of the four directions, but the rock was too small for that many, so only two could be made.

After First Woman had marked two large circles on the slab, they all set to work with sharp flints and stone hammers, cutting out the two equal sized wheels. This was not an easy task, as the quartz was just as hard as the implements with

First Woman has the Sun and Moon fashioned from discs of quartz; the
chips became stars

which they were working, but after a time two round, flat
discs lay shaped and ready for their purpose. Then First Man
and First Woman started decorating the stones in a manner
that would signify the powers that each was to be given. The
first was given a mask of blue turquoise to produce light and
heat, then red coral was tied to the ear lobes and around the
rim. A horn was attached to each side to hold male lightning
and male rain. Feathers of the cardinal, flicker, lark, and the
eagle were tied to its rim to carry it through the sky, and also

to spread the rays of heat and light in the four directions. Four zig-zag lines of male wind and male rain stood at the top and four more hung at the bottom, and four sunspots were placed for guardians who sometimes stood on its face, but more often took their places in the four directions.

"Now it is finished," said First Man, "and I will give it a blessing of mixed pollens, and also a song which will be sung by a lark who hereafter will be known as the 'sun's voice'."

"But this cannot remain here!" stated First Woman. "It must be placed in the sky!"

No one seemed to know how this was to be done until Fire Man suggested that it should be carried to the top of the highest mountain and placed on the tallest peak at the edge of the earth where it could shine on all of the land at the same time. So it was taken to the eastern mountains and fastened to the sky with darts of flash lightning.

Then First Woman and her helpers went back to decorate the second, round stone disc, which was the same size as the first. But First Woman said, "We do not need another bearer of heat and light, so this one will carry coolness and moisture." Then they decorated its face with white shell, placed a band of yellow pollen on its chin, and made a rim of red coral. Magpie, nighthawk, turkey and crane feathers were fastened on four sides to bear its weight and its horns held female lightning and soft winds. Four straight lines placed at the top, and another four at the bottom, gave it control over the summer rains. When it was finished this, too, was taken to the top of an eastern peak and fastened to the sky with sheet lightning.

"Now everyone should be satisfied," remarked First Woman as she looked at the discs. "Now we have light, heat and moisture, all coming from the sky."

But again many of the First People were complaining. "This is not right," they said. "If the sun stays in the east all the time it will always be summer on that side of the land, and it will always be winter on the other side."

"The sun must move across the sky," First Man agreed, "but how can it move when it is only a stone and has no spirit?"

Everyone looked at the two discs and knew that they were just decorated stones with no life of their own, and they wondered what could be done about it. Then two very old and very wise men stepped forth and said, "We will give our spirits to the sun and the moon so they will have life and power to move across the sky." One entered the turquoise disc and he was called *Jóhonaa'áí*, or Sun Bearer; the other entered the white disc and he was called *Tl'éhonaa'áí*, or Moon Bearer. Immediately the two stones began to quiver and show signs of moving.

"But how shall I know where to go or which paths to follow?" asked the sun; and the moon asked the same question.

"The eagle is guided by his tail feathers," said First Man. "We will give you each twelve feathers from the eagle's tail to point the correct paths you are to follow, and the changes in the paths will mark the changes in the seasons." So twelve tall, white feathers were fastened to the top of each headdress to indicate a different path for each month of the year.

Sun was the first to start on his journey across the sky, while Moon waited all day, until Sun had reached the peaks of the western mountains but was still looking back across the land.

At this point Moon queried, "Now?"

And Sun answered, "Now!"

So Moon was about to climb into the sky, when Wind Boy, who had been standing just behind him, thought he would help by pushing with a stiff breeze. This breeze hit Moon Bearer in the back and blew the twelve feathers forward across his face, so he could not see where he was going. All he could do was follow where the tips of the feathers pointed, and, as these were now slanted in different directions, Moon has always followed strange paths across the sky.

First Man or First Woman could do nothing about this,

so everyone went back to the place where they had been working on the slab of quartz. On the blanket which had held the
two large discs were now many small pieces of stone of every
size and shape, along with the dust that the chipping and
shaping had created.

"Look at all this good quartz that is left!" First Man exclaimed.

And First Woman said, "It must not be wasted! We will
use it to make more lights in the night sky."

So again they took their flint knives and their chisels and
stone hammers, to shape the stars that would shine only at
night. There were very few large pieces of quartz but there
were myriads of small chunks, and much stardust by the time
they had finished their work.

When all the stars were ready to be placed in the sky First
Woman said, "I will use these to write the laws that are to
govern mankind for all time. These laws cannot be written
on the water as that is always changing its form, nor can they
be written in the sand as the wind would soon erase them, but
if they are written in the stars they can be read and remembered forever."

After that she drew a sky pattern on the ground and
placed one of the large stars in the north. "This will never
move!" she said, "and it will be known as the Campfire of
the North. It will also be known as the traveler's guide and as
the lodestar." Then she placed large stars in the other three
directions and one in the very center of her sky pattern.
"These must be placed in the sky in their correct positions,"
she told Fire Man, who had shot two crooked fire arrows into
the sky so their trails formed a ladder, and who now undertook the task of placing the stars in their proper locations on
the blanket of night. Before Fire Man picked up the first one,
First Woman had traced in the sand a path for each to follow
across the skyways, and First Man had tied a prayer feather
on its upper point, giving each star a prayer to chant as it
marched along its designated path.

First Man places the large stars in the sky, and thus writes the laws for mankind; Coyote watches

Fire Man began with the north star and continued climbing the ladder until all the large stars were in the sky, while First Woman placed other stars in groups to form the constellations. It was slow work, as there were many stars and the ladder was very tall.

While all this work was taking place Coyote had been standing close by, watching every move Fire Man made. Now he saw one fairly large star still lying on the ground, so he asked First Woman if he might have it for his own. "You may have that star," First Woman agreed, "if you will place it in the sky directly over your mountain. Part of the time it will be quite dim, but when it shines brightly its brilliance will indicate your mating season." So Coyote carefully climbed the zig-zag ladder, clinging to the rungs with one paw while grasping the star with the other, and placed Canopus, which the Navaho call *Ma'ii Bizo'*, in the southern sky directly over Coyote Mountain.

84

The first two constellations designed by First Woman were Ursa Major, which was named *Náhookos*, meaning Cold Man of the North, and Cassiopeia his wife, who was called *Nahookás Ba'ááad*. These two were placed on opposite sides of *So'tsoh*, or the North Star, which was their home fire; they move around this center and never leave it. No other constellation approaches them to interfere with their set routine. This arrangement of constellations established a law that has persisted to this day. This law stipulates that only one couple may live by one hogan fire.

After these, First Woman designed a slender constellation in the shape of two rabbit tracks, one following the other. This is the constellation that governs all hunting, and, during the spring and early summer when the open end points upward, no one may hunt game animals. In the late fall, when the open end tips toward the earth, the hunting season begins. In the days when the Navaho people depended mostly on game for their food, the laws governing hunting were very strict. No hunting was allowed during an animal's mating season nor while the young were still with their mothers; and no deer or antelope under the age of two years were ever killed. Even today the Navaho do not care for the meat from lambs or young kids, and, now that deer and antelope have almost disappeared from Navaho territory and have been replaced by sheep and goats, they use only the older ones for their food, as they believe the meat provides greater strength.

The next pattern to be made by First Woman was one recognized as a man with wide shoulders standing in a stooped position with his hands on his knees in order to support a heavy load of harvest. This constellation, or "the harvester," commands the Dine'é to work hard during the harvest season so they may garner sufficient food for the long, cold winter.

Thunderbird, who carries all the clouds in his tail and all the rains under his wings, was the next constellation, along with Hydra, "the horned rattler," who was given charge of the underground water channels. The task of placing all these stars in their proper places was going slower and slower, for Fire Man could take only a few stars at a time as he climbed the ladder.

Coyote became impatient as he watched this slow process of placing the constellations. He said to First Woman, "This is taking too long! Why do you not permit me to help? Then we would have this work finished twice as fast!"

First Woman answered, "You always make mistakes and then there is trouble."

But Coyote insisted, saying, "I will do exactly as you say and follow the pattern just as you have placed it on the ground."

First Woman was putting two identical stars into her pattern and had named them "the twins." The two lines which marked their paths ran side by side across the sky. She pointed to them and said to Coyote, "Take these two stars and place them somewhat to the west where they will walk hand-in-hand across the center of the sky."

Then Coyote picked up the two identical stars (Gemini), one in each hand, and walked to the ladder. He had seen Fire Man climb the ladder with his hands full of stars, and thought he could do the same, but when he was half-way up he chanced to look down, and the distance was so great that he became dizzy and almost fell. To make matters worse, Wind Boy came whistling by to see what Coyote was doing, and shook the ladder from east to west. Quickly shifting the star in his right hand over to his left which then carried both stars, he continued to climb, using his right hand to cling to the ladder. When he reached the sky he soon found the two places where the stars belonged, but when he looked at the stars in his hand he could not tell them apart and did not know which one went to the right or which to the left. So he closed his eyes and put one star in place with his left hand and the other with his right. Immediately a harsh, grating noise was heard, and he knew they were in the wrong spots and were trying to change places. He could do nothing about it now, as they were well beyond his reach, so he hurried down the ladder while the two stars crossed, one in front of the other, to gain their proper paths. First Woman met him at the foot of the ladder and berated him with angry words and fierce gestures. "Now look what you have done!" she cried. "Those two were supposed to establish peace and friendship among all peoples of the earth. Now they will cause enmity, strife, and dissension that will plague mankind forever. You shall carry no more stars to the sky!"

Coyote grumbled as he walked away, "It was not my fault! Wind Boy shook the ladder and I almost fell off!"

First Woman told him to go away as she was too busy to be bothered, and went on laying out patterns for constellations which Fire Man carried to the sky. There was *K'aalógii*, or Butterfly; *Tsídiitltsoii*, the lark who sang his song to the sun every morning; there was *Na'ashoii*, the lizard; *Ma'ii-* tsoh, the wolf; *Atsá*, the eagle; *Dahsání*, the porcupine, who was given charge of the growth of all trees on the mountains; and the caterpillar. First Woman made many, many more until nearly every animal, bird, and insect had star counterparts in the sky.

As Fire Man bore these up the ladder he carried his fire torch which held burning coals strapped to his left arm, and as each star was put into the sky he gave it a spark of fire to light its path so it could find its way even through the darkest night. All was going very well, but, as Fire Man was carrying a medium-sized star to the east, the straps that held his torch came loose and the torch fell to the ground so he had no spark to give to this star. He placed it in the sky, ran down the ladder to recover his torch, and then hurried back to give it a light, but he could not find it, as it had started to move and had lost its path in the darkness. This is called the "black star;" it wanders here and there and brings bad luck wherever it goes. It sends out little black arrows to cause pain and sickness and, if a person who is traveling at night feels a sharp prick in his shoulder or his back, he will know that the black star is not far away.

When Fire Man returned to earth, First Woman did not know whether to give him another constellation to carry to the sky, or not. Not many stones left on the blanket were large enough to make stars, but many chips and piles of dust remained. She filled Fire Man's hands with stone fragments, and he started climbing; he was halfway up the ladder when he glanced at the stones in his hands and decided that they were too small and too many to place individually, so he gave each one a spark of fire and then, handful by handful, he threw them against the night sky. Here they still may be seen as close groups of small stars which represent the small, fire-carrying creatures of the earth such as the lightning beetle, or firefly, and the glowworm.

As Fire Man was descending the ladder, Coyote stepped up to the blanket and, grasping it by two corners, swung it into the air so the stone fragments and the star dust swept across the sky in a great arc that reached from horizon to horizon. This formed the Milky Way which the Navaho call *Yikáisdáhí*. They believe it provides a pathway for the spirits traveling between heaven and earth, each little star being one footprint.

Then Coyote dropped the blanket and everyone looked at the sky which now was filled with stars. First Woman said, "Now all the laws our people will need are printed in the sky where everyone can see them. One man of each generation must learn these laws so he may interpret them to the others and, when he is growing old, he must pass this knowledge to a younger man who will then be the teacher. The commands written in the stars must be obeyed forever!"

Nowadays, it is only the Navaho medicine men who know the constellations and can explain the laws they represent.

Hosteen Bat sprinkles herbs on the fire of the Fire clans and brings peace to the First Peoples' world

Chapter 9

FIRE MOUNTAIN, THE BAT AND HOSTEEN OWL

DURING THE TIME FIRST MAN was busy placing the stones on the shore and causing them to become high mountain walls to protect the four sides of the land, all the other First People followed him closely to watch how this was done. Among those who kept near him were Fire Man, Coyote Man, and Hosteen Badger. These three kept careful watch and tried to remember every move he made because they wished the other people to believe they were just as powerful as he. It was easy to see what he did with his hands, but they could not tell what kind of pollens he was carrying in his medicine bag, nor what powerful liquid he put into his mouth before blowing on the colored stones to turn them into mountains. This was magic that belonged only to First Man and could not be shared with anyone else.

Fire Man shooting an arrow into the middle of t[

Fire Man was the first of the three to decide to build a mountain, and he said to Coyote, "I cannot build a mountain like those made by First Man, but I can build one in my own way. I shall make mine wide and hollow with many large rooms so all the people of the five Fire clans can live inside. We are many, and we cannot live in a small place."

"I think that is a very good idea," agreed Badger, and Coyote nodded his approval.

Coyote then said, "You build your mountain just the way you would like to have it, and I will help." But Coyote did not intend to help, he simply wanted to watch Fire Man

90

orld, the Place of Burning Pitch, to make his mountain

and learn how it was done for he, too, had decided that he would build a mountain as a home for himself and his family.

Badger offered his assistance, but Fire Man said there was nothing for him to do as no digging was to be done. "I will not need your help," Fire Man told Badger, "for I have my own ways of making holes in the earth." So Badger turned and walked away, wondering how Fire Man was planning to dig holes when he had no sharp claws with which to dig.

Fire Man and Coyote walked eastward until they came to the top of a small hill that stood in a wide valley. "I shall

91

need room for a large mountain," Fire Man declared as he looked around. Then he opened his quiver which held thirteen fire arrows, and, selecting the longest one, he shot it down into the very center of the hill. Down, down it went until it came to the very middle of the world, the Place of Running Pitch, which started to smoke and then to burn when it was hit by the fire arrow. Soon a thin spiral of black smoke came from the top of the hill. Again Fire Man took an arrow from his quiver and shot it into the hill from the east. Then he dispatched three others from the south, the west, and the north.

The earth where these arrows entered began to smoke and then flames flashed into the air, and in a short time four large holes were burned into the sides of the hill. Coyote watched as these grew deeper and deeper, thinking that soon the hill would be nothing but a hollow shell. Finally Fire Man took a bag of white powder and sprinkled a little of it into the four holes to smother the fires. At first a dense black smoke arose and when the wind had cleared that away they knew the fires were out in all except the central hole. Fire Man turned to Coyote and said, "Come with me inside the hill and help me push the roof higher and dig the floor deeper."

But Coyote did not wish to do this so he answered, "I am sorry! I would like very much to help you, but I have just remembered that my friend, Hosteen Badger, is waiting for me. I must see what he wants."

And with that, Coyote ran away very quickly, while Fire Man climbed down into the eastern side of the burning hill to complete his mountain without help from anyone. He followed the slanting path the fire arrow had made in the eastern side, as the central opening was still spouting forth flame and smoke. When he had gone down some distance, Fire Man found that the rock and earth had melted together and were flowing around like hot, brown syrup. This he started shoveling out through the opening in the top of the hill and it ran down the sides, filling cracks and gullies. When this was out of his way, he started pushing the ceiling upward so his mountain grew tall and steep with many sharp rocky pinnacles on the top; when he had pushed on all four sides of the interior, it grew large all around with room inside for all the Fire clans that would soon be gathering there from the four directions.

While Fire Man was building his mountain, leaping flames from the central shaft reached high into the sky, and black smoke filled the air. The ground on which the First People stood heaved and trembled until few could stand upright, and many thought that the end of the world had come. They said to each other, "Fire Man is about to destroy our world and perhaps we had better ask Rainbow to build us a bridge so we can follow the Pueblo people to another place."

Then Coyote came by to tell them not to worry, as all this shaking was only Fire Man building a mountain in which all the Fire clans could live. The First People were not inclined to believe Hosteen Coyote, for he had never been famed for telling the truth, but when Hosteen Badger came ambling along, grumbling about the smoke that bothered his eyes, and told them the same thing, they decided to wait and see what might happen.

"When Fire Man has finished his mountain," Coyote said to them, "he and all the other Fire People will go inside and then our land will stop shaking."

But Coyote was sadly mistaken. The time came when Fire Man had his mountain home finished and invited all his clan relatives to come and live with him. There were four large groups of these relatives, all dressed in black and wearing black masks marked with seven white stars. They all carried quivers with five red fire darts.

The group from the east entered Fire Mountain through the eastern portal and occupied a large room on that side of the mountain; the southern group went inside through the southern tunnel; the western clans used the western tunnel;

93

and those from the north occupied the large room on the northern side. But none of them entered the space around the central fire, as that room was to be used as a council meeting place. Now these Fire clans were no sooner inside the mountain than they began circling around from one place to another to see who had the best place in which to live, and, when the First People listened carefully, they could hear angry voices grumbling and shouting at each other. As black smoke was still coming from the top of the mountain and the land still shook and trembled, they were deeply worried. When it grew dark the smoke turned red, and sometimes the flames leaped high so the First People knew that the Fire People had a very hot fire burning inside the mountain.

Almost the only thing the Dine'é knew about the Fire clans was that their chief business had been that of making war on their enemies. But when they decided to live inside Fire Mountain there were no enemies for them to fight, so they began making war on each other. Sometimes they just quarreled among themselves, trying to find out who was the strongest or who could throw his hammer the farthest; at other times they had battles that shook the earth. These black warriors had fire darts which they did not use on each other, but they also had flint hammers and battle axes which they threw back and forth until it seemed as though they were liable to split Fire Mountain wide open.

Night and day the four Fire clans kept their quarrels going, and it seemed that they never paused, either to eat or to sleep. The people who lived on the earth near them were always in terror lest their own land would split open or perhaps catch fire. It was not at all a pleasant way to live, and they started to complain to anyone who would listen.

"Fire Man did a very bad thing," they said, "when he brought his warring relatives to this new land and built a place for them to stay! There are too many of them, and each clan should have its own mountain. Then there would not be so much fighting. As it is, we are always afraid and have no peace at all!" This was very true and everyone was troubled.

"If only some way could be found to make them stop fighting," First Woman suggested, "our land would stop shaking and we could build our own houses."

First Man added, "But that is all they know how to do! They are all warriors and have no chanters, or medicine men, to teach them other things."

"Perhaps if we sent someone to talk to them and ask them to smoke the peace pipe," said First Woman, "they would listen to him and learn the ways of peace. Perhaps they have never heard of any other way of living!"

All the people who heard these words thought this would be a very good idea, and, as no one had a better plan to suggest, they all said, "We will send someone to talk to the Fire clans, someone who will carry the pipe of peace and ask everyone to take a puff. It will be a promise that all fighting will cease and everyone will be friends."

This seemed like a good plan, but who would go? Who would not be afraid of the dark caves in the mountain sides and of the smoke and fumes that came from the fires below? This was a question no one could answer, as it seemed that everyone was much too afraid of the Fire clans to enter the mountain where they lived. Then First Woman asked all the people to stand in line so she could speak to each individually. It made a long line with big, black Bear at one end and little Bat at the other. When all were in line, First Woman went to each person in turn, beginning with Bear and Wolf, Coyote and Badger, to ask if they would be willing to carry a message of peace to the Fire clans in Fire Mountain. But each one had some good excuse, explaining why he could not go. At the very last, when she had almost given up hope of finding a volunteer, she came to little Bat who was quite sound asleep. He was hanging, head downward, from a low bush and was wrapped tightly in his fur coat with the hood pulled over his eyes. First Woman reached out and shook him until he pushed the hood back and opened his eyes, but he was not very wide awake when she said to him, "Will you go into the deep caverns of Fire Mountain and ask the Fire People to stop fighting and shaking our land?"

Bat snapped his teeth together and answered crossly, "Yes! I will go! It can be no noisier than this place, and perhaps when I return it will be quiet here so I can sleep!"

Now everyone who heard this answer looked at the other in surprise, for Hosteen Bat had the reputation of being a very cranky person and not at all obliging. He kept very much to himself and seemed to carry a grudge against the whole world. He had not always been such a grouch, for when he lived in the lower world his disposition had been kind and friendly. In the Third World, when the weather had started to turn cold and all the First People were choosing coats to keep them warm, he had been asleep in a warm cave. When he awoke, he decided that he would wear a feather coat with long, powerful wings and then he would be a bird. But he was too late making his choice; the feathers were all gone, and so was most of the fur and the shell. A few scraps of thin fur were lying about, so he took these and stretched them to make himself a coat. When he put it on, the others looked at him and said, "Here is another mouse!"

Now this made Bat very angry, as he did not wish to be a mouse, so he searched around until he found a few pieces of thin buckskin which he stitched together to make a pair of wings. When these were fastened to his shoulders, he flew up into the air crying, "Look! Look at me fly! I am not a mouse, I am a bird, and I will live in a high place and not in the ground with the mice!" But the birds would not accept him as a member of their group.

"Where are your feathers?" they cried. "Where is your bill? And where is your tail?" They flew away laughing and left him quite alone. He decided to visit the mice and see if they would be his friends, but when he came near their homes they taunted him, saying, "Look who comes to join us! He is no friend of ours for he thinks he is a bird! He thinks he is better than we are because he can fly a little with those clumsy wings!"

Then someone asked, "What shall we call him now, for he is not a bird, nor is he a mouse?" They thought this over for a time, then someone said, "We will call him Buckskin Ears, for by his own efforts he has earned that name."

That name has never been changed and the Dine'é still call him Hosteen Buckskin Ears. All this disappointment and trouble with his neighbors caused him to become cross and bitter toward everyone, and his disposition has not changed much to this very day.

It had been so long since Hosteen Bat had been friendly with his neighbors that they all were excited when they heard him say he would go into the caves of Fire Mountain. They crowded around him to ask what presents he intended to take to the Fire People, and to advise him to keep away from the smoke and sulphur fumes. Many tried to tell him things he should say to please the fierce warriors. But little Bat paid no attention and started unfolding his awkward wings. "At least these solid wings will not be singed in the heat as would wings made of feathers," he remarked. "And I do not intend trying to please them, I will just tell them to be quiet and stop their quarreling."

Just then Hosteen Owl joined the crowd around little Bat and started laughing at all this advice. "Who! Who! Who could be so foolish as to believe that words will do any good?" he chuckled. "Those Fire People are very fierce and strong. They will never listen to a command from a small, weak person like Hosteen Bat!" He paused to puff out his chest and to be sure that everyone was listening, then he continued, "I am the only one who knows what Bat should take with him!" When he had finished this speech, Owl opened the bundle of herbs, powders and medicines he had brought from the lower world. He took out four things which he gave to Hosteen Bat to use when he reached the home of the fire people.

Bat collects gifts for the Fire clans—beads of turquoise, jasper, shell and jet

First he gave Bat herbs to sprinkle on the central fire to make a sweet, pleasant aroma; second he gave him tobacco for cigarettes that would make the smoker happy; third he gave him medicine to mix with water which would cause any one who drank to become very drowsy; and fourth he gave powder to sprinkle on the food, so those who ate would enjoy wonderful dreams. All this medicine was placed in four buckskin bags, making a large parcel which Hosteen Bat did not know how to carry.

"I will wrap it in a strong silk bag that will not break or tear," offered Mrs. Spider, "then you can strap it on your back." And she wove a web to hold the medicine bags and spun a rope to go around Bat's shoulders.

Hosteen Owl helped him tie the bundle securely to his back, then said to the First People, "This is all little Bat will need to accomplish his mission and this is all the tobacco and herb medicine I brought from the lower world. It contains much magic, and I have given it for the benefit of all the people living in this new land. From now on, these same herbs may be used in any rites where peace is desired." From that time until now, Hosteen Owl has been known as a great medicine man who can perform strange magic, both good and bad.

Now that little Bat had the four medicines safely tied across his back, many other people came to hand him charms, amulets and gifts to take to the Fire People, for they were not quite sure that Owl's herbs would do any good. They gave Bat pieces of turquoise, yellow jasper, white shell, and black jet, all made into beautiful beads. They also gave him a stone peace pipe, a small shell filled with pure water that never grew less, and cakes made of millet meal and sunflower seeds. When little Bat was ready to go Hosteen Owl said, "I will fly ahead of you to show you the way, as my home is not far from Fire Mountain."

It was growing dark when the two started on their journey, and they were guided in the right direction by the glow of a fire that they could see over the top of the mountain where the Fire People made their homes. Soon they were near enough to hear the grumbling and roaring going on inside, but this did not stop them. They knew by these noises that the people of the four Fire clans were all inside quarreling with each other, so no sentinels would be posted to warn them of the approach of the two strangers. They flew around the base of the mountain which here was covered with brush and grass, but found no crack or opening whatever. Then they went a little higher and again made a complete circle, with no better results. The third flight around the mountain revealed no openings, but, up where the rocks were bare and black, Owl saw a wisp of smoke coming from a small crack in the rocky wall. When he flew there he found the crack much too small for him to enter. He put his face close to the opening in order to peer inside; the bitter, yellow smoke hurt his eyes and throat so that he coughed and said, "This crack in the rock leads down to the central room, but there is too much smoke here! We will have to find some other place to enter."

Little Bat, however, was not afraid of the smoke and said, "This is just the place we have been looking for! It is so small they will never think that any person could come through it, and no one will be guarding the other end. You keep watch here and I will go into the mountain."

It was quite true that Owl was much larger than Bat and would need a larger entrance, and it was also true that Owl's feathers would not withstand the heat which accompanied the yellow smoke. So little Bat wrapped a cloud of black mist around his head to keep the smoke out of his eyes, a cloud of blue mist around his shoulders to protect the precious medicine bag, and a cloud of grey mist around his body to make himself appear larger than he really was. With all these wrappings of different colors no one could tell that it was only little Bat walking along toward the Fire People. When he was well wrapped in his robes of mist, little Bat entered the narrow opening and followed a long passage leading down into the mountain. Owl stood peering after him until he was out of sight in the smoky tunnel and said to himself, "This is a very dangerous thing for little Bat to do and he may never come back, but he has my powerful medicines with him and he possesses magic of his own, so I will wait here to see what happens."

All this time he had been gazing into the opening and the yellow smoke had been hurting his big, round eyes. Finally he could hardly see at all, so he flew up to a hidden crevice which was deep enough that he could hide in the darkness.

From that time to this Hosteen Owl's eyes have been bright yellow, and he hides during the day but flies about as soon as it grows dark.

Little Bat walked this way and that in the smoky darkness as the winding path led him down toward the center of the mountain. At every downward step the noise grew louder and louder while all around him the rocks echoed and shook. But he kept on walking and did not stop until he came to a very large room which was filled with people dressed in black, all of whom were shouting and throwing stone hammers at each other. These bounced off the black obsidian armor and did little harm to anyone. When the Fire People saw little Bat standing in the room they were so surprised that they became quiet for a moment. They were not sure what kind of person he could be as he was not black like themselves and, in the flickering glow of the dancing flames, his misty robes appeared to be of many hues. When he threw off his robes they saw that this was an on-earth-person who had ventured into their stronghold. Then they started shouting again, but this time they were shouting at little Bat and threatening him with their hammers. Little Bat felt very frightened as he thought they would shoot him with their fiery darts at any minute, so he hid again in his blankets of mist.

Now the room he had entered was in the eastern part of the mountain and these Fire People were from the east. "I think these people would like jet beads," he thought, and reaching into his medicine bag he took out a large handful of black beads which he scattered across the floor. When the Fire People saw the jet beads rolling across the floor, they stopped looking at Hosteen Bat and each one tried to pick up as many beads as he could grab. This gave little Bat a chance to slip over to the south room. Here again he found a room filled with Fire People who were shouting and throwing hammers at each other. Again the people were greatly surprised when they saw the strange visitor all wrapped in shining colors. Without waiting for them to throw their hammers or fire darts, little Bat spilled a quantity of blue beads over the floor and, while they were busy picking them up, slipped quietly into the west room. The Fire People here were no different from those in the first two rooms, and they were shouting just as angrily while throwing their hammers. They were so occupied with their quarrels that they did not notice little Bat until he scattered yellow beads all about; then they started scrambling after them to see who could get the most, and this gave him a chance to slip into the north room. Here the noise and quarreling were the same as in the other three rooms, so he tossed many white shell beads across the floor and ran into the middle room. Now this seemed to be as large as all the other rooms put together and it held four times as many people.

Deep in a pit in the central part of the floor a great fire was burning and the air was filled with the evil-smelling smoke. The Fire People did not pay him the least notice until he threw a circle of red coral beads at their feet. Then everyone stopped quarreling and looked around to see where the beads had come from, but decided to pick them up first and deal with little Bat later. As they were paying no attention to what he was doing, little Bat took this opportunity to walk close to the central fire and sprinkle it thickly with the herbs from his first package; then he stepped back and wrapped himself in his misty robes. Very soon pale blue smoke carrying a very pleasant aroma filled the central room and drifted through the doors that Bat had left open, into all the rooms in the mountain home of the Fire clans. The people in the central chamber were aware of it first, and then those in the other rooms began to wonder where this delightful fragrance was coming from, and what could have caused it.

They were so curious that, while they were still picking up the beads, they started talking to each other. "What can this be?" they asked. "We have never smelled anything like this before!" Up until now, the only odors that had filled the

Bat passes a peace pipe to the Fire People; beside him is a basket of mush,
a water jug and his gifts

rooms had come from the smoke of the central fire, and had
been bitter and unpleasant, causing everyone to cough and
choke. "Perhaps this is some new kind of magic!" they said
to each other, "let us go into the central room and learn
what can be causing it."

So all the Fire People came crowding into the middle
room to determine what could be causing the delightful new
odor. When they saw little Bat sprinkling something on the
central fire, and watched the spirals of blue smoke arising,
they knew this was the source of the aroma. They said to him,
"This is a very pleasing incense you are putting on our fire.
It makes our rooms pleasant places in which to live. We
would like to have some of your sweet-smelling powder.
Where can we get it?"

"Oh, I can give you all you want," little Bat replied. "I
can get plenty more where this came from," and he handed
them four bags filled with the incense. "Use it as often as you
wish," he told the headmen of each clan. "These bags will
never become empty." Then he added, "I have other kinds
of medicine which you may like even better." Of course, the

Fire People did not know what these could be, so he told them to sit on the floor in a big circle and he would show them.

When they were all sitting quietly in the circle, little Bat took the stone peace pipe that First Man had loaned him and filled it with four varieties of tobacco. This he lighted with a spark from the central fire, took a few puffs, and then handed it to the person sitting at his right, who took a few puffs and then passed it to the next Fire Man. Each one in the circle had eight puffs on the peace pipe and then passed it to his neighbor until all had tasted smoke from the magic pipe. They all looked pleased and nodded to each other and smiled when they said, "Yes, this is better than the first magic! I wonder what more he can be carrying in his medicine bag?"

Hosteen Bat now knew that Owl's herb medicines were very powerful, and he ceased to be afraid of the fierce Fire People, for they did not seem to possess any real magic except fire. However, this was one magic element which the First People did not have. He told himself that he would take a few bright, red-hot coals home with him when he returned to their council meeting. But first he must use the last two packages of medicine that Owl had given him. He took the shell water jar from under his robes and poured all the herbs from the third package into the water. When this was well mixed, he passed it around for the Fire People to drink. Now this shell jar was connected with the bottomless lake so, although every person drank all he could hold, the water in the jar never became less, even after everyone had finished.

"That was a very fine drink," the Fire People all said. "We would like to know where we can obtain a supply for future use."

"You may have this bottle," offered little Bat. "It will never be empty and you can drink whenever you wish."

The Fire People were very grateful and called him a very kind friend. After this they grew very drowsy and leaned against each other to praise the drink and to say how good little Bat had been to bring it them. Then little Bat hastened to open his fourth package of herbs and proceeded to mix them with the mush of wild millet and sunflower seeds that First Woman had given him. He had carried this mush in a tightly woven basket made of reeds and grasses, with a well fitting cover, so it had not spilled. Quickly he passed the food around to first one Fire person and then another, telling each to eat all he desired as the basket would never be empty. It was very good mush and everyone praised it, saying, "We must find out where we can get a supply of this!"

Then little Bat said, "I will leave this basket with you and you will never find it empty."

One by one the fierce Fire People stretched themselves on the floor and fell fast sleep. It was easy to tell by the smiles on their faces that their minds were filled with pleasant dreams.

As Bat folded his robes about him and looked around at the sleeping warriors who had laid aside their hammers and fire darts and had completely forgotten their quarrels, he knew he had accomplished the mission he had been sent to do. So he tied up all that was left of Hosteen Owl's powerful herbs and started walking back up the path down which he had come.

"Perhaps I should take a spark of fire back with me," thought little Bat. "But how can I carry it? If I had not given them the peace pipe I could carry it in that; now I have nothing, so I will try to come again and bring a torch." As he walked along he was thinking that he did not wish the flame to go out while all the Fire People were asleep, for if it did, how would the First People ever obtain fire when they needed it?

Just then he saw Wind Boy coming down the path and called to him, "Do you come this way every day?"

Wind Boy answered, "Yes! I often come through this passage into Fire Mountain, just to find out what is happening here."

Bat was glad to hear him say this and said, "Well then, I will give you charge of the central fire and you must fan it whenever it seems to be dying, so it will burn and burn forever in the middle of Fire Mountain."

"I shall be glad to keep it burning," promised Wind Boy, "and when you see a glow in the sky above it, you will know that I have kept my promise and the fire still burns."

When Wind Boy had gone whistling merrily on his way, little Bat began to walk faster, but the path seemed very long and steep. His feet dragged and he grew more and more weary with every step for he, too, had smoked the peace pipe and sipped the water from the magic jar. Now he was growing very sleepy. Slowly and more slowly, he walked toward the entrance of the tunnel until finally he could go no further. Looking up he saw a ledge jutting from the canyon wall, and above it a curved arch of rock which sheltered a small cave. "What a nice, quiet place that will be now that the Fire People are all asleep," he thought. Climbing up the steep rock, he found a cozy crevice in the roof of the cave, folded his fur blanket around his head, and was soon fast asleep. To this very day, in this place or in some other just like it, you will find little Bat sleeping the daylight hours away, for his eyes were injured by the bitter smoke and cannot endure sunlight.

Hosteen Owl waited outside the mountain passage for a long time. Once he thought he could hear Bat returning along the trail, but it was only Wind Boy coming back from fanning the fire. After this had happened twice, Owl made up his mind to ask Wind Boy if he had met little Bat in the passage.

"Oh, yes!" answered Wind Boy when he was questioned, "I saw him when he climbed to a warm little cave and went to sleep."

Now Owl was sure it was useless to wait longer for Bat's return and he, too, flew away to find a dark hiding place where the light would not hurt his eyes.

The First People never saw either Bat or Owl in the day-time after that, but as the land had stopped shaking and as no more grumbling noises occurred from under the earth, they came to the conclusion that Hosteen Owl's herbs had been very powerful and that little Bat had succeeded in quieting the fierce Fire People.

Hosteen Badger building a mountain for his home

Chapter 10

HOMES FOR COYOTE AND BADGER

AFTER COYOTE HAD REFUSED to help Fire Man finish his mountain, he ran away very quickly to find Hosteen Badger who was walking around looking for some hillside into which he could dig a deep hole to use as his home. Every time he came to a mound of earth Badger would walk all around it wondering if it might be large enough to furnish the shelter he needed; then, after deciding that it was too small, he would ramble on seeking something larger. When the two met, Coyote asked, "Why are you walking around this rough country? What are you looking for?"

And Badger replied, "I am looking for a hill or mesa that is large enough for me to burrow into and build myself a house."

"You will find nothing but hummocks here," Coyote

told him. "The only way we will have homes that are warm and safe is to build our own mountain."

Hosteen Badger had never thought of building a mountain, but Coyote had watched First Man when the four sacred mountains were made, and had been with Fire Man when he started his mountain, so now he thought that he could easily build one for himself. However, one thing he needed he did not have, and that was a rock which had been brought from the lower world.

He said to Badger, "If you can bring me just one rock from each of the sacred mountains in the lower world we can build a mountain of our own."

"But how will I get those rocks you think you need?" asked Badger.

"You must go to the people living on the mountains and ask for them," replied Coyote, who then curled himself into a ball and went soundly asleep, knowing that Hosteen Badger would not be back for a long time.

Now Badger was not nearly as simple-minded as some people believed him to be. He knew that he would never be given a rock from any of the sacred mountains unless he had something to give in payment. So he thought for a long time; then he dug into the ground under a bush and found a nest of fat grubs. These he took in his cheek and went to the home of Hosteen Owl and said, "Mr. Owl, I hear it said that you have very keen hearing. Will you please give me a tiny ball of wax from your ear? I have brought you a nest of fat grubs as payment."

"Very well," answered Hosteen Owl, and he rubbed his right ear until he had a soft, round ball of earwax which he gave to Badger in return for the nest of grubs. Badger wrapped the wax in a wide leaf and hastened away on another errand.

This time he went to a rim of rocks and searched along the side until he found a hole where bees were going in and out. This he knew was a beehive, and, reaching into the hole, he broke off a section of honeycomb dripping with golden honey, which he took directly to the home of Hosteen Bear and exchanged for two hairs from the bear's nose.

Now Badger had two of the gifts he needed for his trip to the four sacred mountains, but he needed two more. Quickly he ran to the valley where many bushes grew and found a patch of groundcherries which he picked and wrapped in a spider web; then he hurried to the home of Mountain Sheep, plucking a jointed reed as he went. Mountain Sheep was fond of ripe cherries and was willing to pay for them with a dribble of tears from his far-sighted eyes. Badger sealed the tears into the reed and started on his fourth and last mission.

He then went to a smooth rock and dripped a little honey on its flat surface, and it was not long until a swarm of flies was buzzing over the honey. When a number were trapped in the sticky stuff, he killed them all and put them in a milkweed pod, then went quickly to find Hosteen Turtle. He told Turtle, "I have many sweet flies for your dinner if you will go to the lily pond and bring me a large, fat lily bulb." This was very easy for Turtle to do as his home was among the lily roots, and soon the exchange was made.

It was a great distance to the white peaks that guarded the edge of the land on the east. Badger was not a fast runner like Coyote, so darkness had fallen when he came to the door of white Wolf's den. Now the two guardians of these mountains were white Wolf, who was in command during the night, and Bald Eagle who kept watch during the day. These two ruled all the living creatures on their mountains with fierce strictness and did not welcome strangers into their midst. White Wolf heard Hosteen Badger's approach some distance away, and went to meet him.

"Who are you who comes in the dark to steal something from our mountain?" he shouted at Badger, while his eyes glittered like green emeralds.

"I have not come to steal anything at all," replied Badger,

who also possessed night-eyes. "I have come to ask for a favor."

"We do not grant favors to beggars," Wolf replied.

"I did not expect you would!" said Badger. "So I have brought you a gift in exchange."

Now white Wolf was always ready to accept presents, so he said in a milder voice, "What is this favor you have come to ask, and what is the gift you have brought in exchange?"

"This is a very precious gift I am bringing," Badger stated. "Let us go inside your house where no one will be listening." So they went inside white Wolf's den, and Badger looked all around the walls and the ceiling to see if there were any rocks. He saw clay and brown earth and sand, but no rocks of any kind. Then he asked Wolf if he had any chunks or pieces of white rock like that which had been used to build the mountain.

"No," answered white Wolf, "my home is built of brown earth and hard clay."

Badger was disappointed but decided that clay would be better than nothing so he said, "I have a ball of earwax that was given me by Hosteen Owl, who has the keenest hearing of anyone in the whole world. Anyone who puts this wax in his ears will be able to hear the slightest sound made at a great distance."

Now everyone knew that Owl could hear better than anyone else, and Wolf was eager to own the earwax. "You can have anything you see," he told Hosteen Badger.

Badger pointed to a large lump of white clay lying on the floor in one corner and said, "I will exchange this earwax for that lump of clay."

"Oh, no!" exclaimed white Wolf, "I cannot give you that clay, for my wife needs it to make a pottery bowl. I think you had better choose something else!"

But Badger would take nothing else, and finally the clay was wrapped in a grass mat and Hosteen Wolf accepted the earwax.

Badger walked all the next day to reach the blue mountain in the south. Again it was night before he came to the den of blue Fox who was chief of the night on this mountain. Bluebird, who was chief during the day, had just finished his watch and gone to his home in a tall pine tree. Blue Fox heard Badger coming and went to meet him, as he wished to see who could be approaching this late at night. When he saw that it was only his friend, Hosteen Badger, he asked, "What brings you here at night when all people are supposed to be asleep?"

Then Badger told him that he had come to ask a favor, as he was looking for a rock from the center of the mountain.

"I cannot give you rocks or any part of this mountain," stated blue Fox, "for this belongs to all of the people and not just to me."

Then Badger pleaded, "I have a very wonderful gift for anyone who will give me a rock or a ball of clay from this mountain."

This interested blue Fox and he looked around slyly. "Come inside," he invited, "someone may be listening."

So the two went into blue Fox's den and this time Badger was looking for a piece of blue rock, but none was to be seen. However, a large piece of blue clay was lying near the south wall. "If I cannot find a blue rock, then clay will have to do," thought Badger as he said to Fox, "I have brought a reed filled with tears from the eyes of a mountain sheep and anyone who puts them into his eyes will be able to see from one mountain to another, all the way around the world."

Now blue Fox desired nothing more than to be able to see long distances so he said, "What is it you want in exchange for the reed?"

I would like the chunk of blue clay that is lying near the south wall," Badger replied.

"Oh, no!" Fox exclaimed, "That is pottery clay and it belongs to my wife."

But Badger would have nothing else although Fox offered him several things. So blue Fox finally gave Badger the blue clay in return for the reed filled with tears.

Again Badger walked all day, this time in a westerly direction, and it was long after dark when he came to the cave of Hosteen Puma who was the nighttime chief of the western mountains, while yellow Warbler reigned during the day. Badger was puffing and grumbling as he walked along for he was growing weary of all this traveling. So Puma was aware of his approach and stepped down from his cave to greet him saying, "This is a strange time for visitors to come calling! What can be so important that it brings you here in the dark?"

"I come on a very important errand," replied Hosteen Badger. "Everyone has been building mountains to serve as their dwelling places, and now Coyote and I are planning on building one for ourselves. I have come here to get a piece of yellow rock to help build our mountain."

"There are no yellow rocks here on the west mountain," Puma replied, "and I could not give them to you if there were."

Then Badger said, "I have a wonderful gift for anyone who will find a yellow rock for me."

Puma was curious to find out what the gift might be so he said, "Come up to my cave and we will talk this over."

Badger climbed to Puma's cave and looked all around but could discover no stones of any kind. However, a solid piece of yellow clay was lying near the west wall.

Badger was disappointed for he knew now that he would never find any stones, so he turned to Puma and said, "I am carrying two hairs from the nostrils of big silver Bear that lives on Chuska Peak, and whoever places these hairs in his nostrils will be able to scent enemies from a great distance."

If Puma desired one thing more than all else it was to be keen of scent, so he said to Badger, "What is there in my cave that you would take in exchange for the two hairs?"

Then Badger pointed to the lump of clay and said, "I would like to have that piece of clay!"

Puma was not pleased at this request and said, "I cannot give you that as it belongs to my wife, and is the only piece of yellow pottery clay in this world, as she brought it from the lower world." Then Puma asked Badger to choose something else, saying that here was a bundle of canary feathers he might like, or there was a bowl of sunflower pollen that would make plants grow.

But Badger only shook his head and pointed to the lump of clay.

Finally Puma walked over to the clay, picked it up, and handed it to Hosteen Badger saying as he did so, "Use as much as you please, it will never become any smaller."

Badger gave him the two hairs, then, leaving the cave he walked a little way to find a place to sleep.

The next day he journeyed north, and it took him all day to arrive at the Big Sheep Mountains which were ruled over by Magpie and Porcupine. Now Badger and Porcupine were cousins, but they were not fond of each other as both were easily angered; and when Badger had called Porcupine a thief, Hosteen Porcupine had retaliated by filling his face full of sharp quills. Badger did not care to visit Porcupine, but he needed a red stone or a lump of red clay to take to Coyote, so he went to Porcupine's den and asked to be admitted.

The door was opened a little way and a voice asked what he wanted. He answered, "I have come to get a red stone or a piece of red clay so Hosteen Coyote can build a house."

The same voice answered, "I have no red stones and I cannot give you the clay for it does not belong to me."

Then Badger volunteered the information, "I am carrying a wonderful gift for the person who will hand me the lump of red clay."

It was well known that Porcupine was a very inquisitive

person, and he simply had to know what Badger was carrying. So the door opened slowly and Badger showed Porcupine the fat lily bulb he had brought from the lake. Porcupine was also a greedy glutton and he dearly loved sweet lily bulbs, so he did not hesitate long before handing Badger the lump of clay and grabbing the bulb.

Carrying the heavy pieces of clay, two under each arm, Badger returned to the place where Coyote had been sleeping, but Coyote was not there. Now Coyote had decided to look for a piece of land on which to build his mountain. He knew this would not be easy to find as few of the First People would accept him for a neighbor, and he did not care to associate with other ones. So he had pretended to be asleep when Badger started on his journey, for he had no desire to travel all around the world in search of the four rocks. As soon as Badger was out of sight, Coyote walked slowly about, seeking some lonely spot where he would not be bothered or spied upon by anyone. When he came to a bare area south of Fire Mountain, which had been denuded by the molten rock that Fire Man had thrown out of his home, Coyote thought, "This is just the place. No one will bother me here!" So he picked up a stick and started making an outline for his mountain.

Badger did not know where to look for Coyote, so he walked along asking everyone he met, "Have you seen Coyote today?"

They all answered, "No, we have not seen him," until he came to Lizard who lived near Fire Peak.

He answered the question with, "Yes, I saw him just a few minutes ago some distance south of Fire Mountain. He was acting very queerly, making marks on the ground with a long stick."

As soon as Badger knew where to go, it did not take him long to find his friend. Sure enough! Coyote was walking about scratching the ground with a stick, but he looked up when Badger said to him, "I have been to all four sacred mountains where the Pueblo peoples live, and I have brought you four chunks of pottery clay with which you may be able to build your house."

When Coyote heard this he was quite angry, as he had wanted rock for his building material, so he said, "Why have you brought me this clay? It is good for nothing!"

Then Badger told him, "This is very beautiful clay and it seems to be almost as hard as stone. It was brought from the lower world by the Pueblo women who use it to make their pottery. No more of it is to be found in this world and it is magic; no matter how much you use, it never diminishes in size."

Then Badger placed the clay on the ground in front of Coyote who now looked at it with greater respect. "Is this all there is?" he asked.

"It is all there is of these colors," Badger replied, "but in the three other mountains the women still have brown, grey, and pink clay with which to make their pottery."

"Perhaps this will do even better than rock," Coyote mused. "We will see what we can do with it." Then he set to work with his stick, re-marking the ground in a design for an odd-shaped mountain. He marked a large circle in each of the four directions and then he divided each lump of clay into four sections. Patting each of the sixteen pieces into thin, round discs, he placed a white disc in the center of the eastern circle, a blue disc in the southern, a yellow one in the west, and a red one at the north. When this was done, he placed a second layer of disks over those already in place, being careful to use opposite colors. Again he changed colors as he put a third layer on each mound, and finally, the last four discs were put in place on top of the others. Then he looked around for loose brown earth to sprinkle over and around the four mounds in order to disguise their colors, for he was afraid someone would try to steal the clay.

The mounds of colored clay were all standing at some distance from each other, and Coyote planned to have them grow so tall and wide that they would merge into one large mountain, but how this was to be done he did not know. He knew that First Man had taken some powerful medicine in his mouth to blow onto the tops of the four sacred mountains to cause them to grow tall, and then he had taken something else in his mouth to blow on two sides so they would stretch along the edges of the land. But who could tell him what this magic medicine was or where he should go to obtain the amount he needed? Coyote sat down to rest and plan what he should do. He knew the medicine came from the lower world as that was where all magic was created, but he was too proud to ask First Man to tell him how he could get it or to beg to be given a little.

"Now who still lives in the great ocean?" he pondered, "and who seeks his food along the slopes of the submerged mountains?" This brought to mind Hosteen Seal who had once been an earth person, speaking the earth language, and who often sunned himself on the beach beyond the yellow mountains of the west. Coyote stood up and said to Badger, "I know just the person to bring us the growing medicine from the mountain under the ocean. It is Hosteen Seal. But I cannot leave these mounds I have built or someone will steal the clay, so you must go and ask Seal to get some for us."

Badger was not pleased at being sent on another long journey and replied, "I am tired. Why do you not go to find Hosteen Seal while I stay here to guard the clay; after all it belongs to me just as much as it does to you."

Then Coyote replied, "I would just as soon go, but I cannot let you act as guard, for you would sleep most of the day and not hear the thieves if they came; while I sleep with my eyes, I keep my ears open."

"If I must go," grumbled Badger, "you must give me a present to give Hosteen Seal in exchange for his magic medicine."

Coyote thought for a while and then said, "I have heard

that Seal is very fond of soft music; perhaps Nightingale will give you a song to take as a gift."

So Badger took a basket of tiny berries to Nightingale to exchange for a song, and when the bird had tasted the berries she said, "Yes, I have a brief song I will give you," and she snipped the tips off two white feathers on her throat. She said to Badger, "Anyone who wears these two feathers near his ears will aways hear sweet music."

Badger tied the two small feathers in the hairs of his neck and started off on the long journey to the western mountains, and the ocean beyond. It was a wearisome trip but he finally arrived at the rocky beach where the seal family was basking in the sun. There he untied the song feathers and approached Hosteen Seal, who opened his eyes to say, "What strange person is this who comes to disturb my afternoon nap?"

Then Badger said, "I have come from the other side of the yellow mountains to ask a favor."

Hosteen Seal was only half awake, "Well, speak up!" he snapped. "What is the favor you wish to ask?"

Badger held out the tiny song feathers which were emitting a soft trilling sound and said, "I have brought you bird songs to exchange for a reed filled with magic growing medicine from beneath the dark waters."

Seal shook his head, then said, "The medicine for magic growth belongs to Whale who is the largest creature in the ocean, and he will not give it away."

"Then we must find out what he would like most and give him a present for some of it," declared Badger, "for I cannot return to my home without it."

"Hosteen Whale is very fond of perfume," Seal stated. "He will share his magic with us for a vial of some unusual scent."

"I will see what I can find," said Badger. Then, cutting a section of hollow cane grass, he went to the mountainside where shrubs and tall bushes were growing. He had not walked far when he became aware of a very sweet aroma coming from a high bush around which many bees were flying. "This is just what I am looking for," thought Badger as he pulled the branches down in order to reach the sweet smelling flowers, and filled his reed bottle with pollen from the honey locust tree. Seal took the small bottle and dived to the bottom of the ocean where he found Whale lying on a bed of sea moss.

"I have come to ask for a favor," Seal stated as Whale stared at him. "I would like to have some of the magic medicine that makes you so large."

"Ho, ho! So you want some of my magic!" boomed Whale. "Well I have none to give away, so you need not beg for it."

Then Seal took the stopper out of the reed bottle of honey locust pollen and waved it in front of Whale's enormous nose.

"Hah, what is that pleasant smell?" asked Whale as he peered here and there with squinted eyes.

"It is perfume from mountain flowers," answered Seal, "which I will give you in return for a conch shell filled with your magic medicine." Seal had brought a large conch shell with a roll of seaweed for a stopper.

Whale was loath to part with even a small portion of his magic, but he was delighted with the locust perfume, so he finally filled the shell with medicine from a sack he carried in his throat, and gave it to Hosteen Seal.

Seal tied the open bottle of pollen to the hairs in Whale's nostril and then swam back to the shore. He came to the place where Badger was waiting and handed him the shell saying, "Here is the magic medicine which will make anything it touches grow to a thousand times its former size."

Badger took the conch shell and handed Seal the two feather tips, saying as he did so, "Put these into your ears and you will always hear the soft music of singing birds."

After saying good-by to Seal, Badger started the long

Coyote builds his mountain home while Badger rests in the background

homeward journey; he arrived at the four clay mounds late one afternoon, footsore and very tired. Coyote, who had been watching his approach, ran to meet him and spoke crossly, "What delayed you? Why have you been gone so long? The warm weather is nearly over and I have no house in which to live! Did you bring the magic medicine?"

"Yes," Badger replied, "I have brought the medicine, but it was a very long journey and I had to climb mountains and cross deserts; that is why it took so long." Then he handed Coyote the heavy shell.

"So this is it at last!" exclaimed Coyote. "Now we shall see how much magic it possesses!"

But Badger was too exhausted to care what happened, and looked around for a nook or small cave where he could sleep.

Coyote removed the stopper from the shell and then filled his mouth and approached the four mounds of clay. After blowing some of the mixture across the top of each mound, he stood back to see what would happen. Slowly the mounds grew up and up until they resembled four slim domes pointing toward the sky. Then Coyote circled each one, blowing the medicine on every side; but when he came to the last one he did not have enough liquid in his mouth to complete the north side. The first three turned into large, round hills, the bases of which met in the center. This did not suit Coyote who had planned to have them so large they would all join together and form one big mountain.

"I will use the remainder of the magic fluid," he thought, "and spray them again." But when he went to the place where he had left the shell he found that it had tipped over, and, because he had forgotten to replace the stopper, the magic fluid had run down a small ditch which had then turned into a deep arroyo. "Now look what you have done!" he scolded Badger. But Badger was fast asleep behind one of the clay mountains and did not hear a word Coyote said. These clay hills never grew any larger, and one was always crooked on one side; but they are still to be seen where Coyote built them, and they are still called Coyote Mountain because they resemble the four pads of a coyote's paw.

When the mountain was finished, Coyote looked at it and was very proud to know that he had built such a fine place for his home. Then he began to wonder how he was going to get inside. He walked around looking for a door in the wall, or a cave, or even a narrow crevice of some kind, but could find no entrance whatever. All four hills were just hard, smooth, pottery clay that had turned to rock in the dry air. "This mountain is not going to do me much good unless I can find some way to get inside," Coyote said to himself as he walked round and round the base of the mountain.

Now a good many other people had noticed these new peaks and had decided to find out who had made them. Coyote saw Hosteen Skunk coming toward him and as soon as he was near he said to him, "I have made myself a house of clay but the door has been hidden behind the covering of dirt. Dig into the mountain on this side and I will dig on the other until one of us finds it."

So Skunk started to dig on the east and Coyote ran to the south where Badger was sleeping. "Wake up! Wake up!" he called to Badger, "and help me find the door to my house. You dig on this side and I will dig on the other until we find it."

So Badger started digging on the south side of the mountain, and Coyote ran to the west where he sat down to wait for whomever might come to that side. Soon he saw Gopher approaching and called, "My friend, I am glad to see you! I have built a house but the door has been hidden by the dirt, please dig on this side while I dig on the other until one of us finds it."

As Gopher started to dig, Coyote ran to the north. There he saw blind Mole walking slowly along, so he told him the same story and blind Mole agreed to dig on that side. Now four people were working, and each of them thought that Coyote was digging on the opposite side of the mountain, but Coyote was a person who never worked if he could find someone else to do it for him. So he climbed to the highest peak and watched as the loose dirt came flying out of the holes where his friends were trying to locate the door of his house. After a long time, he went down and walked into the tunnel that Hosteen Badger had dug in the south side of

Skunk, Badger, Gopher and Mole are tricked into digging four doorways
for Coyote's new home, while he watches them work

the mountain. He found that it went all the way to the
center, and there his friends had worked round and round
to make a large room. He thought he would thank them for
making him this fine place to live, but Skunk, Badger,
Gopher and Mole were all fast asleep, for they were very
tired from so much hard digging. Coyote laughed and said
to himself, "Four doors are much better than one; my
friends have truly served me well, and I now have a house
which is better than I had expected." From that day to this,
Coyote has built his home with two or more entrances.

When the four workers awoke, Coyote forgot all about
thanking them for the work they had accomplished, but said
to them, "You have slept a long time in my house, now you
must go to your own homes!"

Blind Mole, Skunk, and Gopher did not like this large
room; they thought it much too cold and draughty, so they
ambled away to find something smaller.

But Badger had expected to live with Coyote and he did
not know what to say. However, he was a good natured chap

123

and refused to argue with Coyote, so he crawled out of the tunnel he had dug and sat at the entrance wondering how to go about building a home of his own. Suddenly he remembered that his back had been covered with black mud when he had dug the passage from the lower world, and rubbing his hand along his back he found that every hair was stiff with dried earth.

"I believe I will have enough earth from the lower world with which to start," he said to himself. And he carefully scraped his back until he had a long roll of black dirt in his paws. Walking a little distance from Coyote Mountain, he molded this roll of dirt into a long ridge, then, remembering that he had carried Coyote's clay under his arms, he felt of the under arm hairs, and, sure enough, they were thick with clay. Carefully he loosened every particle and made a roll to place on top of the earthen ridge. Badger had taken care to note where the growing medicine had spilled and had soaked into the ground. Going to this place, he stooped and scraped up a big pile of the wet earth to place on top of the clay. As he worked, the ridge began to grow upward and sideways, so when he had finished a long, high mesa existed on which he could make his home. Coyote Mountain and Badger Mesa are well known to all Navaho, and the story of how they were built is told to visitors who are interested in Navaho tales.

First Man finds Snail's water bottle and sprinkles pollen on the water
trickling from it, making a great river

Chapter 11

SNAIL BRINGS PURE WATER

GRADUALLY, THROUGH THE GUID-
ance of First Man and First Woman, and with the assistance
of Fire Man and the four Wind People, this Fifth World in
which the First People now live, was becoming a safe and
pleasant place. When they had first arrived it consisted of a
wide mesa completely surrounded by low, uneven land,

buffeted on all sides by fierce tempests and high tides and traversed by hungry monsters. Later, mountains guarded the coasts and prevented the angry waves and the sea beasts from marching across the land. The land monsters had disappeared and warmth and sunshine prevailed during the day, while the moon and stars glorified the night. All this had been brought about by the industry of all the First People and the bravery of a few.

With all this accomplished, this world still was not much like the one from which they had been driven by the flood. There were no trees on the mountains, and no springs, creeks, or rivers of running water anywhere. The only water was in the lake that had formed at *Hajíínái,* or the Place of Emergence, and it was muddy and did not taste fresh. Of course the water in the ocean was too salty to drink. The people remembered the springs and the clear rivers that had furnished water for everyone in the lower world and they complained, one to another, about the lack of pure water.

"How can we live here?" they asked First Woman. "Where are the rain clouds, and where is the good, pure water we need to keep us alive? If we drink from the muddy lake we will become ill, for it is filled with things that have been drowned, and it would be still worse to drink the salt water of the great ocean."

First Woman listened to these complaints, but she had no answer for this problem. She knew it was all too true, for no one could live very long in a land where no pure water was to be found.

First Man, who had been a Waterway chanter in the lower world, had already recognized their need for a permanent supply of pure water, and he said to the assembled people, "If anyone here brought a water bag, or a wicker water bottle, or even a hollow reed filled with good, pure water from the lower world, bring it to me. I have magic medicine which will cause it to change into a bubbling spring that will form a swift, clear river so there will be water enough for everyone." As he said this, he glanced around the circle looking for an answer from first one group of people and then another, but no one replied.

Now four kinds of people had come from the lower world to live in this new land. The Sky People who had wings and could fly through the air came first, next came the On-earth People who walked on the surface of the earth. Then came the Under-earth People who built their homes in caves or in tunnels in the ground, and last of all came the Water People who lived in, or near, the water. When First Man asked for a jug of pure water everyone immediately turned to look at the group of Water People, thinking they were the ones who should have brought at least a little pure water in some sort of container. They glanced inquiringly at Beaver, Otter, Turtle and Frog to see what they would have to say. However, these four shook their heads, saying that they were sorry, but they had wished to bring so many other things from the lower world that they did not think it would be necessary to bring water.

Then everyone looked at Crane and Grebe, Duck and Loon, but these four also shook their heads saying, "How could we carry water on our flight to the sky? We flew all the way for there was no room for us inside the reed."

Now First Woman wondered if someone could be hiding a piece of hollow reed filled with water in his bundle, so she went from one to another asking to see what each had brought. She found that they had food and clothing, seeds and planting sticks, medicines and ornaments, cotton and dye stuffs, but no water at all.

The First People were quite alarmed by this time and began to wonder how they would be able to live in this new land. First Woman did not give up so easily for she believed that there must be moisture somewhere, if not on earth, then in the sky. She asked the Sky People to fly as high as they could and try to discover a little cloud or a veil of mist which they could bring to First Man to use as seed for creating rain. They said they would try, and Bluebird flew toward the east, Finch to the south, Cardinal journeyed west and Magpie flew toward the north, while Lark flew upward, straight as an arrow, toward the zenith. These messengers were gone a long time but finally returned carrying no bit of cloud, no strand of mist, nor even the smallest drop of water.

Now it was the On-earth People's turn to look around and see what they could find. Those who started on the search were the Ute in the north, the Apache in the east, the Zuni in the south, the Hopi in the west and the Navaho in the center. They searched in the canyons, at the foot of each high promontory, along the sides of the mesas, and high on the mountains, but they had no better luck than the others. Then the Under-earth People explored the caverns, the tunnels, and the crevices to see if a little water might be stored beneath the surface of the earth. Everywhere they looked the ground was dry and the rock was smooth and hard. By this time all of the First People were becoming quite discouraged as it seemed they would never have any water except from that muddy lake.

"First there was so much water that we nearly were drowned and now we suffer because we have none at all," they complained.

But the Wise One spoke to them saying: "There is only one place to go for good, pure water and that is deep down under the great ocean where a spring of clear, clean water comes up from under the lower world mountains. Someone must go there and bring back the pure water we need in this new world."

First Woman asked, "But how can anyone bring pure water while swimming through the salty ocean?"

"I will make a water bottle in which the water may be carried," stated First Man. From his bead necklace he took a long line of white shell beads, and sealing one end, he coiled them around and around on each other like the coil of a squash tendril. Then he blew into the open end so the beads stuck together, and the inside opening grew larger and larger. When he thought that the shell bottle was large enough to hold the amount of water he would need, he made a stopper of red coral to close the mouth. When he had finished, he tied a cord of rainbow around the bottle's neck; then he said, "Here is a white shell bottle that can be taken to the bottom of the ocean without being harmed. Who will be the one to take it there, fill it with good, pure water and bring it back to our new land?" First Man looked at the Water People who were standing in a group at one side of the circle.

Brown Otter was the first to step forth when First Man finished speaking. "Let me go for the pure water," he offered. "I am a very fast swimmer and I am strong enough to carry the heavy bottle after it has been filled."

"Otter will go! Otter will go!" cried all the First People. "And he will bring us the pure water we need."

But grey Beaver, who had been standing just behind Otter and did not wish Otter to receive all the attention of the crowd, stepped in front of First Man to say, "I will go with him and help carry the water bottle so we can return twice as soon as one person going alone. Also I can guard against dangerous enemies."

"That sounds like a good plan," First Man replied, and he tied a magic spear point to Beaver's tail.

Otter took the shell water jug, slipped the loop of rainbow rope around his neck, and the two dived into the deep water of the great ocean. As they went deeper and deeper they saw many things that were growing from the rocks and ledges. There were mosses and ferns, and bright colored vines, and the roots and bulbs of water lilies, watercress, bulrushes and cane grass, all of which would be useful to the people of the new world. Otter said to Beaver, "I think we should gather some of this and plant it where it will be of use to us."

But Beaver was looking at the roots of the willow, the birch, the tamarac, and the witch hazel, thinking that if these grew in the new land the bark would make good food, so he answered, "We will make bundles of these roots and bulbs while we are here, and if we plant them at the edge of Muddy Lake, I think they will grow."

So Otter laid the shell water bottle on the ledge and started gathering the roots of water plants to wrap around his body, and bulbs to carry on his back. Beaver made bundles of tree roots and clippings to take back to the homeland.

Many of the people were waiting for them and when they saw the two wading toward the shore they said, "Now who can these two strange people be who come walking across the beach?" For Otter and Beaver looked so queer, all wrapped in roots and vines and with bundles of sticks tied to their backs, that no one could recognize who they were. But as they came nearer First Man exclaimed, "Look! They are the two who went for the pure water, but how strangely they are wrapped!"

"Yes, we are the two who went into the ocean with the white shell bottle; but see what wonderful things we have brought back with us!" And Otter showed them the bulbs and roots. "I have brought you bulbs and lily roots which we will plant in the new land, and Beaver has roots and sprouts of all kinds of willows and sedges which will grow along the banks of Muddy Lake."

"But where is the water? Where is the good, pure water?" shouted all the people with one voice.

Then Beaver hung his head in shame as Otter said, "We did not bring it! We forgot about it when we saw all these things growing under the water. We thought it would be better to bring this food."

"But where is the water bottle? Give me the water bottle!" First Man demanded. "I must find someone else to bring us the pure water."

Otter answered in a small voice saying, "We left it lying on a rock near the water plants; we forgot to bring it back."

Now this was indeed bad news, for if the water bottle was lost or broken there would be no way to bring the good water to the new world. All of the First People looked at Otter and Beaver wondering how they could have been so careless, while First Man said, "You have failed to do as you were told and for that you must be punished. Take these roots and bulbs and sprouts you have brought and plant them in the shallows of Muddy Lake, and there you shall build your homes and hide when other people come near. But the things you have brought will prove useful to many people in many ways, so we shall give you charge of all waters in lakes and ponds from now henceforward."

Then First Man asked who would volunteer to go into the water to find the shell bottle and then bring back the good water they needed. Two young men stepped forward saying, "We will go! We are fast swimmers and can stay under water for long periods of time." These two were dressed in similar garb, one wearing a brown coat with a yellow vest and the other a green coat with a white vest. Their names were Hosteen Turtle and Hosteen Frog.

"Very well," First Man told them, "we will be waiting here for your return."

Together they dived into the water and soon approached the place where the bottle was lying. "I will carry it part of the way," offered Turtle. "Then you can take it." So Turtle picked up the bottle and Frog helped tie it on his back. Now Turtle was not a large person, and the thick shell bottle was long and heavy, so he was forced to stoop over and walk on all fours to keep it from dragging in the mud and sand. There was no smooth path to follow as they made their way over sharp stones, sticks, and pieces of broken shell. Turtle's yellow vest was soon in tatters and his skin received many scratches. In the meantime, the ropes that tied the water bottle to his back loosened so it shifted from one side to the other with every step he took. "This will never do," said Turtle to Frog. "You take the water bottle while I stay here and glue together some of these pieces of shell to make a hard coat to protect my back and another to cover my chest."

So Frog took the shell bottle and continued his journey to the spring, but he, too, found the water bottle unwieldy and difficult to carry. His knees bent above his back and his shoulders sagged. "I cannot carry this much further," he thought as he struggled onward. Just then he came to a wall of rock which he could not cross. "This is as far as I can go," he decided, and he removed the red stopper from the shell bottle and let it fill with water that came from under the rock. This water was green with bits of moss, algae, and tiny water bugs, but Frog did not know this, so when the bottle was full he replaced the stopper and started on the home journey.

When he came to the place where he had left Turtle, he was quite surprised at his friend's appearance. Turtle was now wearing armor of yellow shell to protect his chest and stomach, and brown shell to cover his shoulders and back. The shell scraps he had used were not all of the same color or size, but he had glued them together in a beautiful pattern. "I will now carry the bottle," he offered, "as my new coat will prevent me from being hurt." It was high time that Hosteen Frog was relieved of his load, for his knees were bent and his eyes were bulging from his head. Turtle's shell was slippery, but with much pushing and pulling the water bottle was finally tied firmly, and the two continued on their journey swimming toward the shore.

As they came to the beach and walked out onto the land, they both went on all fours. Turtle could not stand upright because of the heavy bottle he was carrying, and Frog did not stand up because he had cramps in his knees.

All of the First People ran to meet them crying, "You

have brought the water! You have brought the water from the bottom of the ocean!"

"Yes, here is the water," Turtle answered as he untied the ropes which held the bottle in place; but Frog said nothing, for he was trying to hide behind Hosteen Turtle.

Then First Man asked, "What took you so long? You have been gone several days!"

"It was a long journey," Turtle replied, "and I stopped to make a suit of armor for myself so I could carry the bottle." Then he handed the water bottle to First Man.

First Man removed the red coral stopper and smelled the water in the bottle. "What is this?" he asked. "This does not smell like good, pure water!" Quickly he poured a little of the liquid from the jar onto the ground where all could see.

"That is not pure water!" everyone exclaimed. "Look at the green moss and the weeds and the water bugs that are in it!"

"This is just dirty water from the bottom of the ocean!" First Man was very angry as he thought that Turtle and Frog had tried to play a trick on all the First People. Picking up the shell water bottle, he walked to a low swale some distance from the ocean and emptied the water on the ground, then blew across it four times. The water spread out into a pond, forming the center of a boggy swamp that reached back to the high cliffs, where sedge, willows, bulrushes, and water lilies were soon growing.

He looked at Turtle and Frog, who were standing close to each other, and said, "From now on this is where you shall make your homes. Because you brought us stale water you must live in places where the water is stagnant. Turtle must always wear his shell coat, while Frog's eyes will always bulge and his legs will always be crooked. But because you brought the shell bottle back from the bottom of the ocean, I will make you rulers of all fens and marshes and shallow waters." This is why we now find frogs and turtles living in

Snail brings water from under the ocean; a hole is worn in his water bottle
and leaking water starts a shining brook

swamps and bogs where the water is filled with moss, and lily
pads cover the surface.

Now, indeed! All the First People had grown discouraged!
When all the best swimmers among the Water People had
failed to bring water from the bubbling spring who else
would be able to do it? They said to each other, "Perhaps it
would have been just as well to have drowned in the lower
world instead of coming to this new land where we may die
of thirst! What can we do now? Is there no one else who will
volunteer to go for the pure water?"

Timidly, little Snail, who was standing near the end of the
long line of Water People, stepped forth and said in a small
voice, "Let me try to bring the good water from the spring at
the bottom of the ocean."

The First People all looked at each other and said, "He
can never do it! He is much too small, and the shell bottle is
larger than he!"

But First Man answered him saying, "Anyone has a right
to try!" So he gave Snail the large water bottle and helped
him tie it on his back. They all watched as little Snail walked
slowly into the water. He did not try to swim; the load on his
back was much too heavy, so he just walked along underwater

very smoothly and carefully as he did not wish to lose the bottle. This was not a fast way to travel and it took him a long time to reach the center of the ocean where clear, pure water was bubbling up from the lower world.

By the time he arrived at the spring, little Snail was very tired from dragging his feet through the mud; he decided to rest a while before starting his long journey home, so he curled up and went to sleep. When he awoke, he felt much better and carefully filled the white shell bottle with clear water from the spring. When it was full, he pushed the red coral stopper in tight so it would not jar loose on the way home. He tried to walk a little faster, but the bottle was heavier now that it was full, and again he plodded slowly along the ocean floor.

When little Snail disappeared in the water, all the First People sat in a circle to await his return. They wondered why First Man had allowed him to go, when better and stronger swimmers had failed. They waited and waited, and after a while they began to think he had lost his way, or perhaps some water monster had swallowed him. "It is of no use to wait here," they told each other. "He will never come back for he has been gone too long! Surely something has happened to him!" So they all went back to their homes, very sad and discouraged.

Some time later, tired little Snail came out of the water with the heavy water bottle tied safely to his back. He looked around for the people who he had expected would be waiting for him, for he had no idea of the length of time he had been away. He wished to give the jar to First Man and he needed someone to help untie the rainbow cords, but everyone had gone and he did not know where they might be. Now little Snail was too tired to walk upright, so he bent almost to the ground as he toiled under his heavy load along the winding path that led upward toward the homes of the First People. As he moved slowly along, the water bottle dragged on the ground, and finally a small hole was worn in the end of the shell. As this hole grew larger, a trickle, and then a small rill of pure water ran out of the jar, followed his winding path down the slope to the ocean; immediately it increased in size to form a clear, bubbling brook. Little Snail struggled up the slope until he came to the crest of the hill. Then he began to realize that the water jar was not as heavy as it had been, so he removed the stopper and peered inside.

Oh! How sad little Snail was when he found that most of the water he had brought from such a long distance had escaped through the hole in the end of the shell! Now he did not wish to see any of the First People, and most of all, he did not wish to see First Man. He put the shell jug down on top of the hill, where the remainder of the water ran out and formed a small pool. Seeing that the water bottle was now completely empty, he decided it would make a good place in which to hide. He crawled inside and pulled his blanket over the opening, never once looking back at the shining trail that he had left behind. Then, being a very tired little fellow, he soon was fast asleep.

Now First Man knew that little Snail had always been a very slow person, so he decided to go back to the edge of the ocean and see if he might have returned after everyone had departed. When he reached the water he saw no sign of little Snail, but he did see the clear shining brook that led from the ocean to the top of a distant hill. This had not been there when all the people were assembled to watch little Snail start on his mission, so First Man knelt by the stream and tasted the water. "This is truly good, fresh water!" First Man exclaimed. "Now I know that little Snail has come from the bubbling spring in the center of the ocean floor, and has with him the white shell water bottle full of good, pure water!" Then he walked along beside the brook, sprinkling it with the pollen he had gathered from the bulrushes, singing the water chant as he went. Behind him the shining brook changed into a wide river of sweet water which wound its way down the slope to empty into the ocean.

After a time, First Man came to the top of the hill and there he saw the white shell bottle with little Snail's blanket drawn over the opening, and he knew that little Snail must be inside. Then he saw the small pool of water made by the last trickle from the jar, and this he sprinkled with a handful of water pollen, and a large spring gushed out of the ground near the spot where the water jar was lying. He said to himself, "Now the First People will have all the pure water they need, for here is a great river flowing across their land, and above it is a gushing spring whose waters feed the river."

About this time little Snail awoke and peered out from behind his blanket to see what was happening, and to find out what was making the singing noise that had awakened him. When he saw First Man standing beside the shining water of the bubbling spring, he was ashamed because the shell bottle contained no water. He did not know that the spring was made by the water he had brought from the ocean.

When First Man saw little Snail peering out of the shell, he called to him and said, "You have done a very helpful thing by carrying out the mission on which you were sent. The pure water which you have brought from the ocean has made us a wide river and a spring, the waters of which will never fail. From now on, the white shell water bottle will be your home and you shall carry it on your back to protect you from your enemies. Wherever you walk you will leave a moist, shining trail to remind people of your gift to them. You shall be the guardian of all springs and will make sure that nothing ever stops the water from flowing, or makes it impure. In return for your efforts, all Earth People will think well of you and you will never be harmed."

In this world, the First People lacked fire; Coyote stole it for them from Fire Mountain

Chapter 12

COYOTE BRINGS FIRE

WHEN THE FIRST PEOPLE CAME to the present Fifth World, the daylight lasted three times as long as the darkness, and no seasonal changes took place. No differences occurred between the temperatures of the days of spring, summer, autumn, or winter, so the people were never too cold or too warm. But after the sun, moon, and stars had been placed in the sky, the days and nights became of equal duration, and the four seasons were established. This variation of weather was caused by the eagle feathers fastened in Sun's headdress to indicate the paths he should follow. These feathers stood close together, but each one pointed to a different path the sun must follow; the two in the center pointed almost straight from east to west, but the five on one side slanted toward the north, while the five on the other side slanted to the south. After this, the weather was no longer as pleasant as it had been, for part of the time it was too warm and then it became too cold.

This was very hard on the First People who had no warm hogans, or stone houses, in which to live; their brush shelters and shallow caves had served as comfortable dwellings up to this time. They all started complaining about the cold, but no one knew what to do about it. Even Coyote, who was now living in his new home in Coyote Mountain, found it much too cold. When he went outside and sat in the sunshine he was warm, but when he went inside his den was so chilly that he shivered and shook. "What can I do about this?" pondered Hosteen Coyote. "My house is not of much use to me when it is too cold to live in! If I could have only a small spark of fire from Fire Man's mountain, it would heat my house and I would be warm." But Coyote did not care to make the journey to Fire Mountain, as he never did anything for himself if he could find someone else who would do it for him. He thought perhaps he could find another animal who would go on this errand. Then he decided to visit the homes of some of his friends and see how they were getting along, now that the weather had turned so cold. He circled around the mountain to the homes of Badger, Skunk, Gopher and Mole, all of whom lived in caves not too far away. When he came to Badger Mesa, he found that Hosteen Badger had used a flat stone to cover his door and keep out the cold wind. Coyote pushed this aside and entered the passage to the cave. He walked along to a small room where he found the Badger family warm and snug in their tiny home. Five of them lived there, and the heat from their bodies warmed the small space so that it was quite comfortable.

"Close the door as you come in!" Badger directed when he saw who was standing in the opening.

So Coyote went back and pulled the stone over the doorway. "Do you know it is growing colder and colder every day?" he inquired.

"Yes," answered Badger, "that has been going on for

some time now, so I have stored a quantity of roots and tubers in my storeroom, blocked my door, and made a warm nest of grasses and leaves."

"But what am I to do?" complained Coyote. "My house is large and the cold wind blows in one door and out another until I am afraid I will freeze!"

"That is because you wanted such a large house," replied Badger, "a small house would be much warmer."

Then Coyote said, "I think we should have fire to warm our homes. Will you help me get a spark of fire?"

Badger shook his head. "No, I do not need fire," he replied. "We are warm enough without it, and the smoke would hurt our eyes."

So Coyote left the home of Hosteen Badger and went to see if Hosteen Skunk knew of some way to get a spark of fire. When he came to Skunk's house he found the door blocked by a great mound of leaves. Making a tunnel through the dry leaves, Coyote peered into the den through the open door. He saw Hosteen Skunk, his wife, and at least a dozen little skunks. The little room was so packed with people and leaves that Coyote did not try to enter. He called to Hosteen Skunk. "My friend," he said, "do you know that the days and nights are growing colder and colder and we may all freeze if we do not get a spark of fire to keep our houses warm?"

Skunk looked at Coyote and said, "Come in and pile the leaves over the opening behind you."

But Coyote could see there was no place for him in that small room and, besides, he did not like the stuffy smell. He said to Skunk, "Will you go with me to Fire Mountain to obtain a spark so all the people may have fires in their homes?"

Skunk looked very cross when he heard this suggestion. "No!" he snapped, "I will not go to Fire Mountain, for I do not need a fire in my house! We have plenty of leaves which make excellent beds and soft coverings, so we are never cold."

Coyote knew he could never persuade Skunk to go on this errand, so he shuffled through the leaves and went to Gopher's home. But there he found no door at all; any openings that might have been were covered by mounds of loose sand. However, he knew Hosteen Gopher and his family were inside, for he could hear them moving about and he could hear the crunch of the nuts they were eating. "Let me in," he called to Gopher, "I wish to talk to you!"

Gopher replied, "I cannot let you in from this side as the sand would fill my house. You will have to dig your way through the tunnel."

Coyote looked at the mound of loose sand and decided that he did not care to dig a path to Gopher's door so he said, "Oh, all right! If it grows colder and colder and you are about to freeze, do not blame me! I am only trying to bring you a spark of fire."

But Gopher began to laugh. "I will never freeze!" he declared. "I have a warm home filled with ferns and moss and I have a large storeroom filled with pine nuts and seeds that will last until summer returns."

Sadly Coyote turned away. He seemed to be the only one who had saved no food for the long winter months or prepared a warm bed for the chilly nights. He knew that blind Mole would be fast asleep by this time and no amount of noise would waken him, so a visit to his house would be quite useless.

Now that these friends had refused to help him, Coyote wondered where he could find a helper. He would need someone who could run swiftly or someone who could fly through the air. Then he said to himself, "Of course! Why did I not think of this before? The birds are the messengers I am going to need! They can fly to the top of Fire Mountain, snatch a burning fagot and return before the fire dies. I will go to the bird colony and find someone who is willing to go!" Greatly cheered by this plan, Coyote trotted away toward the south to visit the Bird People.

As this was the first cold season to visit the Fifth World, the Bird People were not prepared for it, and had no plans for moving further south. However, their part of the country was in the south and was not as cold as the northern part. Even so, the days were growing short and the nights were chilly. Hosteen Owl and Hosteen Eagle did not mind the cold weather, but the little songbirds, who had lived on pollen and grass seeds all summer, were much concerned. Hummingbird, Bluebird, Finch, and Canary had called all the members of the bird colony to come to a meeting and try to decide what they should do. All the summer songbirds were there, and many of those who lived in the reeds and bushes by the lake.

Four only did not come: Eagle, Owl, Magpie and Bluejay. They all had warm homes and did not fear the cold weather.

While the small birds were doing a great deal of chattering, who should come hurrying along but Hosteen Coyote. "Why are you all gathered here?" he demanded.

Finch answered, "We are worried because the days are growing shorter and the air is becoming colder and colder."

"Yes," agreed Coyote, "I have been worried about the same thing." He shook his head. "But I think if the birds will help me we can all be warm again."

On hearing this, the birds clustered around Coyote to learn how they might assist him; they thought he had some plan to make the days warm and sunny again. Then Coyote said, "One warm place exists in this land, and that is the country near Fire Mountain. If we can get a live ember, or even a spark, from the top of that mountain, we will be able to have heat in our homes and we will all be warm, even though the days grow colder and colder!"

The Bird People did not think this would be a very good idea as their houses were built of sticks, grasses, and moss. Many shook their heads and turned away, but others stayed to ask questions.

"Where is this fire?" inquired Flicker, "and how can we get it?"

Coyote had his answer ready. "It will take someone who has strong wings and can fly very fast," he stated. "He must carry a long fagot in his talons and fly to a place above Fire Mountain. Then, when a tongue of flame shoots up toward the sky, he must dip one end of the fagot into the flames, and, when it blazes, he must hurry home before it goes out."

"That does not sound like a difficult thing to do," Flicker decided after careful consideration. "Make me a fagot to carry and I will try to bring back a small flame."

When Coyote heard this he was quite excited. He hurried away to tell the First People that Flicker was willing to fly to the top of Fire Mountain in order to bring everyone a spark to start their fires. "But first we must make him a good solid fagot," he told the listeners.

Then many went to the dry reeds near the lake and started shredding the stalks into thin strands. When they had a long bundle of these, they took more strands to wrap round and round them until they were encased in a tight wrapping from one end to the other, with just a plume of shreds at one end. "Here is a fagot," they said, "that will catch fire easily but will burn slowly." Then they all went with Coyote to give it to Hosteen Flicker, and to see him start on his journey.

As First Woman handed him the bundle she said, "You must be very quiet when you approach the top of the mountain, for Fire Man will be very angry if he sees you stealing his fire and he may shoot fire-arrows at you."

Now this was something Coyote had not mentioned when he had asked Hosteen Flicker to go on the errand, but Flicker had started and he did not turn back. Up and up he flew, and away to the top of Fire Mountain where he remained high in the air waiting for a flame to blaze upward. He glanced around the top of the mountain and saw many large, round boulders lying near the edge of the firepit, but he did not know that two of these were not rocks; they were the grey *Do'tsoh* beasts that had been placed there by Fire Man to guard his precious fire. These big white-faced flies had enormous, protruding, lidless eyes, each eye being composed of dozens of small eyes that could see in every direction at once. As they were never all closed at the same time, the Do'tsoh were on guard night and day.

These guards saw Flicker as he hovered above the mountain, but they made no move until he swooped down to light his bundle of fagots. Then they whirred their wings rapidly so sparks flew high into the air. Sparks from the grey Do'tsoh hit Flicker under the right wing and sparks from the brown Do'tsoh hit Flicker under the left wing, scorching the feathers so they turned bright red. Flicker has red feathers under his wings to this very day. When the sparks hit him, Flicker was so surprised that he dropped the bundled fagot and flew down to the nearest bushes to hide. As no one followed him, he continued his flight to the place where the First People awaited his return.

He told his story to First Woman and ended by saying, "It was not Fire Man who threw the darts at me, as he was not there. It was someone hidden in the rocks near the edge of the pit."

"Someone is guarding the fire," First Woman decided. "I wonder who that can be? Did you see anyone moving about?"

"No," Flicker replied, "I saw nothing except odd shaped boulders."

The First People talked together saying, "This is queer! We must find out about this!"

First Woman asked, "Who has sharp eyes and powerful wings and is willing to go to the top of Fire Mountain to discover who is guarding the fire?" As she spoke she was looking at all the Bird People and she saw *Ginítsoh*, the hawk, standing at one side. Pointing toward him she said, "You are the one to go, as you have strong wings and the keenest vision of anyone except Eagle, who is not here."

Now Ginítsoh was a very vain person, dressed in a bright feather robe, with long wings and a beautiful white tail. He was quite pleased that First Woman had selected him as the scout best equipped to go on this errand. He strutted in front of the other birds saying, "I will go, but I will not bring back a tiny spark of fire! I will bring one of Fire Man's blazing arrows!" Then he stretched out his long wings and was soon out of sight.

When Ginítsoh, the hawk, came to Fire Mountain he circled high above it for some time but could see nothing except the boulders Flicker had described. Dropping a bit lower he continued to circle as he studied the edge of the firepit, but still he could discern no living creature. "This is queer," he said to himself, "something must have made that odd hissing noise and then sent up the showers of sparks!" So he flew some distance away and swiftly came back close to the ground.

This sudden return took the two Do'tsoh by surprise and they were slow in stretching out their short, stubby wings to whir and send the sparks upward. During this pause, Hawk had time to get a good look at the monsters that guarded the fire. He was so surprised at their appearance that he slowed his speed, and the cloud of sparks came up and hit his beautiful, white tail feathers. He did not pause, but kept flying until he was back among the assembled people; he did not know that anything had happened until he heard the shout-

"Your tail is red! Your tail is red!" they were all screaming as they pointed to his tail feathers. When Hawk looked at his tail, he found that every one of his twelve beautiful, white tail feathers had been scorched to a yellowish red. From that day to this Ginítsoh has been known as the Red tail hawk.

When Hawk had told his story to First Woman and had described the two who guarded the fire, no one could think of anything more to do. Coyote had been waiting to see whether the birds would succeed in their mission, and he had heard everything they said on their return. Now he stepped forth and asked Hawk, "Did you say that these guards had large eyes?" When Hawk said they did, Coyote asked, "And did you say that their eyes had no lids?"

Then Hawk answered, "I was quite close to them and I could see no lids on their eyes."

"If that is true," Coyote said, "I think I have a plan by which I may be able to bring the fire we all need."

"Tell us! Tell us!" cried all the First People. But Coyote shook his head. "No, I cannot tell you for if it fails you would all be disappointed." Then he asked to have a long fagot made and tied securely to the end of his tail.

When this had been done, Coyote, ran to the salt marsh that bordered the great ocean and searched among the reeds and grasses for salt crystals that had formed on their stems. He gathered a large handful of crystals which he placed in his left cheek, and then he gathered another handful to place in his right cheek. After this he looked all around near the water until he found several brightly colored shells. When he had all he thought he would need, he turned and trotted away from the ocean toward Fire Mountain. He did not travel rapidly as it was a long journey for anyone on foot, and he wished to save his strength for the homeward dash.

Dusk was falling as he climbed the steep upper slopes of the mountain and came near the grey Do'tsoh that was guarding the east. At intervals flames blazed high above the firepit, lighting the mountain slopes on every side. Coyote waited until the flames had died away and then approached the guards, shaking the shells, which he had strung on a bit of seaweed, and singing in a low voice:

I am the restless Coyote; I wander around, I wander around!

I am the inquisitive Coyote; I wander around!

I am the mischievous Coyote; I wander around, I wander around!

When the two Do'tsoh heard the soft tinkling of the shells and the low voice of Coyote, they both came to the east side of the firepit to watch his approach. "Who is this that comes so boldly up our mountain?" they cried. "Do you not know that we can end your life with one volley of our fire-darts?"

"Yes! I know," answered Coyote, "but I have come as a friend and I have brought you a marvelous gift."

"We have no friends," the two replied. "And if you come nearer, you will be killed!"

Coyote stood still, but he continued shaking the shells to make fairy music, and said, "Listen! Do you not hear the voice of cool, running water and softly shifting sands?"

Now, for a very long time, the two Do'tsoh had been there on the mountain where the heat was intense and the rocks were hard. The thought of cool water and soft sand was very tempting. The brown Do'tsoh said, "How can you bring such things to this place?"

And Coyote answered, "I have them here in my hand as a gift to you. Every time you shake these shells their music will bring moisture, and the rocks will turn to soft sand."

"What do you want in exchange for these magic shells?" the Do'tsoh asked.

"I ask for nothing in return," stated Coyote, "only to be allowed to stand near your fire and warm my back. Night is falling and I am growing cold!"

"I see no harm in allowing you to stand near the firepit until you are warm," agreed one Do'tsoh, and the other made no objections. So Hosteen Coyote stepped between the two and stood with his back to the fire. "Now give us the magic shells," demanded the two guards, but Coyote moved slowly as he was waiting to hear the crackling that would tell him the fire was rising. It was only a moment until he heard the rush of fire inside the mountain, but the Do'tsoh had heard

Coyote steals fire from Fire Mountain and rushes homeward with

the same sound. "Come away from there!" they cried. "You are too close! You will be scorched!"

Now Coyote was quick to act. Holding out the two strings of shells he said, "Here are the magic shells, come and get them!" As the guards came near to grasp the shells, he spat the salt brine from his left cheek into the eyes of the Do'tsoh on his left, and the brine from his right cheek into the eyes of the Do'tsoh on his right.

"Oh! My eyes! Oh, My eyes!" screamed the two as they rolled over and over in pain.

By this time the flame from the pit was rising high in the air and Coyote swished the fagot through it; he then started

ming tail setting fire to the country side; Fire Man's arrows sail in pursuit

leaping down the mountainside. Fire Man had heard the cries of his guards and tried to halt Coyote's flight by shooting four fire-arrows at him. As these were magic arrows they always hit their mark, but Coyote had been warned about them and he ran in a zig-zag path which hid him, first behind one bush and then another. He held his tail out so the fagot at the end caught the arrows and Hosteen Coyote was not harmed. However, this angular course delayed him, so the fire he was carrying burned the fagot closer and closer to his tail, until he could smell the hair beginning to scorch. With a last wild dash across the mesa, he stopped in front of First Woman. "Here is your fire," he panted. "But cut the ties quickly or my tail will be burned." Squirrel snipped the bindings with his sharp teeth, and the flaming sticks fell to the ground where they were quickly picked up by the people who wished to build fires in their homes.

Coyote looked sadly at the tip of his tail which once had been as white as that of Hosteen Fox, but now was burned black. From that day to this, Hosteen Coyote's long bushy tail has been tipped with black.

White Crane carries Frog toward Fire Mountain to quench the fire Coyote
had started

Chapter 13

FROG CREATES RAIN

WHEN COYOTE STARTED RUN-
ning down the side of Fire Mountain with the blazing fagot
tied to the end of his tail, he did not look back to see what
was happening behind him. He was much too concerned
with dodging Fire Man's arrows. As he leaped from bush to
bush, he knew his zig-zag trail would waste precious time,

and he would need to use his greatest speed to reach home before the ties that bound the fagot burned away and the fire was lost. He did not know that every dry bush caught a bit of blazing reed and was soon burning brightly. But Fire Man, who had been trying to destroy him with fire-arrows, noticed the pieces of blazing twigs flying through the bushes and laughed to himself. "Hosteen Coyote has stolen some of my fire," he chuckled, "but stolen things often cause a great deal of trouble; and soon everyone is going to be very sorry he did this, I think. In a little while they are going to have all the fire they need and more than they know how to manage!" Then he gathered up his arrows and went back to his home in the mountain.

At every jump Coyote made, as he zig-zagged down the steep mountain slopes, sparks and blazing bits of reed flew out of the bundle tied to his tail. Little Wind Boy was pleased with these bright new toys, and puffed out his cheeks to blow flaming sticks and leaves high into the air and far across the slopes. Soon, here and there, as far as one could see, clumps of grass and small bushes started to smoke and then burst into flames. Wind Boy danced and whistled around the blazing bushes until he succeeded in spreading the fire all around the mountaintop, and sent it creeping down toward the dwellings of the First People.

For a time, none of the First People noticed the fire on the mountain, as they were busy picking up the burning sticks that fell from Coyote's fagot, and lighting others to carry to their own homes. During this time each small blaze on the mountain was growing larger and larger. Finally Cardinal came flying swiftly and cried, "Look! Look up the mountain! I flew all the way around it and fire is everywhere! Once I flew too near and it turned my feathers red!"

First Woman looked at the mountain and saw leaping flames encircling the top, with some creeping down the sides. She turned to Cardinal and said, "From now on, your feathers will be bright red, and you shall be known as the firebird."

Then she listened to the frightened people as they talked to each other. "Look how the fire is burning all things that grow on the mountainside!" they exclaimed. "Soon it will spread and come down here and then we shall be destroyed!"

"This has happened because Coyote stole fire from Fire Man and did not know how to carry it properly," stated First Man. "After this, when fire is to be moved from place to place, the one who carries it must obtain a hollow stalk of cane that has grown under water, cut four joints, and fill them with moss. The cane will not burn, and the moss will hold the fire for a long time." And this is the way fire is moved from place to place to this very day.

"What can we do to put out this fire?" asked First Woman as she looked around at the assembled people.

Up to this time, no one had known much about fire. They had seen the flames leaping from the top of Fire Mountain and they knew that these flames were the source of both heat and light, but they were so fierce that no one dreamed they could be tamed and used to benefit mankind. Now they were equally afraid of the bush fires on the mountain and no one could suggest a way to quench them.

"Water will put them out," stated First Man, "but there is no water on that mountain."

"What shall we do? What shall we do?" the others asked each other. "How can we take water from the deep lake or the swift river to the mountainsides to stop this fire? Someone must carry it, but how can that be done?"

"I will make a water bottle that can be filled and taken to the mountain," First Woman promised.

Then they all went to the edge of the lake where the reeds and cane grasses grew tall, and there she made a water bottle of woven reeds thickly plastered with clay. This she filled with water from the lake; then she braided a rope of water lily roots to serve as a carrying loop. "Now who will take this bottle to the mountain and pour the water on the blazing bushes?" she asked as she looked toward the place where the Bird People were standing.

"I cannot go," declared Mockingbird, "for the smoke would hurt my throat and I would never sing again!"

"I cannot go," said Nighthawk, "as the smoke would hurt my eyes and I could not see to catch the insects I hunt at dusk!"

"I cannot go," stated Canary, "as the smoke would soil my beautiful feathers!" Then she flew away to gather weed seeds for her children.

Just then a plain, grey bird stepped in front of First Woman and said, "I will take the bottle of water and pour it on the blazing bushes. I have no sweet song that might be ended, nor do I have night-eyes that might be dimmed. As far as my feathers are concerned, they are deep grey and a little smoke will not harm them." Then looping the lily root cord around her neck she flew quickly to the mountain where every bush was then on fire. First she poured a little water on one blaze, next she flew to another and poured water on that. Every time she flew low over a burning bush the fire felt hot on her breast and she could smell scorched feathers. But she did not pause, for she knew this must be done quickly. From bush to bush she flew until all the water was gone and the bottle held not another drop. When little Robin found that the water bottle was empty, she looked around and saw that many bushes were still burning and she was very discouraged. Dropping the bottle, she started beating out the fires with her wings. This was of no avail as she simply succeeded in sending the sparks flying in every direction, so she slowly flew back to where the First People were waiting.

"Did you quench the fire?" they asked.

"Only a small part of it," she replied. "And I lost the water bottle when it became empty."

"You are a brave bird," First Woman said, "and you have burned the feathers of your breast! From now on, your feathers will not all be grey, for you shall wear a bright red

vest, and you will be the one who brings us spring showers."
So that is how little Robin earned the name *Tsídiitlchi'i,* or
Madam Redbreast.

"Little Robin has done the best she could, but the fire is
still burning!" exclaimed the people. "Not enough water
was in the bottle to put out the fire," First Man said. "Someone else must go; perhaps three or four will go at the same
time so as to carry more water." First Man and First Woman
asked all of the Bird People and all of the Insect People if
they would fly to the mountain with water bottles to quench
the fire, but none of them was willing to go. "We are too
small and the fire is now burning all the way around the
mountain," they said. After that they asked the bear, the
lion, the wolf, the lynx, and all of the hunting animals if they
would try to quench the fire, but none thought they could
do anything about it.

Now First Woman had only the Water People left to
ask, and she thought that perhaps some of them would know
a better way of doing it. So she went to the great spring where
little Snail had his home and said to him, "Little Snail, you
are in charge of the water from all the springs; can you take
some of it to Fire Mountain and quench the fire which is now
burning on all sides?"

Little Snail heard the question and would have liked to
help the people who were now in grave danger. He thought
for a while and then answered, "No, I cannot go to the mountain with water to quench the fire, for I am a very slow person
and must always carry my house wherever I go. Then, too, if
I leave my spring the water will cease to flow, and it will fill
with evil-smelling mud so no one can drink here. I am sorry
that I cannot help you!" Then little Snail crawled back into
his shell and pulled a blanket over the doorway.

First Woman turned away from the spring and ran to
the great river where Otter had his home under a rocky bank.
Calling to him, she said, "Come out, Friend Otter, I wish to
ask a favor of you!" When Otter appeared at the door of his

den she said, "We know that you have much water here in this swift river. Will you take it to Fire Mountain to quench the fire that is destroying everything there?"

Hosteen Otter considered this for a minute and then said, "I would like to help you, but first I must go to talk with Hosteen Beaver whose house is built under water not far away." Then Otter trotted away to find Beaver, who said, "Let us call Mink and Muskrat to talk this over." When all four were gathered near First Woman to hear her request they asked, "How will it be possible for us to take this water to the burning mountain?"

"You must turn the direction of its flow," she replied.

"Oh! No! We cannot do that!" exclaimed the Water People, "for if we do, all the land on every side will dry up and become a sandy desert where nothing will grow except cacti and thorn bushes, and if the river was dry we would have no place to live!" So the Water People refused to share the water of their river, and First Woman decided to visit the lake where Hosteen Turtle had his home. She knew he had protected himself with a deep shell that was shaped like a bowl, and she thought he might use this to carry water to quench the fire.

As she approached the lake shore, she saw Hosteen Turtle lying on the soft sand warming himself in the bright sunshine, and, seeing that he was asleep, she made a sharp hissing noise like the voice of Water Snake to awaken him. When he opened his eyes she said, "We know that you have charge of all the water in this large lake. Will you take some of it to Fire Mountain to quench the great fire that is burning there?"

Turtle stretched out his head to see who was talking. When he saw First Woman he said, "What did you say? I do not hear very clearly when my head is inside my shell." First Woman repeated her request but the slow-witted turtle was a long time deciding on an answer. Finally he shook his head and said, "I would like to help you, but if I should take my lake and pour it on the mountain, it would cause a great flood which would wash everyone out into the ocean, and that would be as bad as the fire." Then Hosteen Turtle pulled his head into his shell and went back to sleep.

First Woman was quite discouraged. She had been unable to get water from the spring, or from the river, or from the lake. Now where could she go to get the water she needed to quench the fire on Fire Mountain? She could think of only one more place where she might go to ask for water, and that was at the deep swamp where Hosteen Frog made his home among the roots of the water lilies and bulrushes. She ran very fast now, as the fire was creeping down the sides of the mountain almost to the place where some of the First People had their homes. When she came to the edge of the swamp she called, "Friend Frog! We know that you have enough water here in this deep swamp to cover the whole land. Will you take some of it to Fire Mountain to quench the fire that is burning there?"

Hosteen Frog raised his head out of the water and saw First Woman standing among the reeds waiting to talk to him, so he swam out and sat on a lily pad. Once upon a time, Hosteen Frog was tall and strong, with a pleasant face and straight legs, but now his legs were crooked, his back was humped, and his eyes bulged from his head. But he still wore a beautiful coat made of green mosses, a vest of white lichen, and gloves of bright yellow; and he was considered something of a dandy. In one way Hosteen Frog was a most unusual person, for he wore two coats. One was the usual coat of hide common to most Water People, but the outer coat was woven of porous material that was much like a sponge. It was capable of soaking up vast amounts of water and holding it until Frog squeezed his coat and released the water. Sometimes he would squeeze out a bit of moisture so that he would be concealed by a blue fog, and sometimes he would squeeze harder and a pool of water would appear all around him.

First Woman knew of his ability to carry water wherever he went, and so she spoke to him very politely. "We all know that you are a magic person and have control of all marsh water. If you will take some to Fire Mountain and quench the fire burning there, we will all be very grateful for your kindness."

Hosteen Frog considered this request soberly with his eyes fixed on the sky, then he asked, "What kind of a fire is this?" First Woman told him that it did not leap very high, as the bushes were not tall, but that it was wide and had encircled the mountain. Frog thought about this a moment and then croaked, "I think I can! I think I can!" Making a long leap, he landed in the middle of the pond and disappeared under water. At first no one could see him, and then the water in the pond grew lower and lower so that First Woman and all of the Bird People who were standing among the reeds saw him swimming in the center of the lake, soaking up all the water he could carry. When the pond had become much smaller, Frog swam to the shore and said to First Woman, "You see I am now carrying the water which can quench the fire. Now who will carry me to the mountain? I cannot fly and, if I walk, I will arrive much too late!"

First Woman looked at the large water birds that were standing among the reeds and asked, "Who will carry Hosteen Frog with his load of water?"

They all looked at him saying, "How can we carry him? Our claws will make holes in his coat and then the water will all run out."

"I can find a way by which he may be carried," stated First Woman, and she gathered strong lily roots to weave into a harness with loops on both sides. Then she asked, "Now who will carry Frog to the mountain?"

"Let me try!" cried Kingfisher who grasped the loops in his talons and tried to lift Frog into the air. But, although he flapped his wings wildly, he could not lift him from the ground.

"Let me try!" screamed Fishhawk, when he saw that Kingfisher had given up trying. Fishhawk was larger and had longer wings, but succeeded in moving Frog only little distance from the shore.

"Let me try!" laughed Loon, who was larger than the others and often carried big fish in his talons; but he did not get much further.

Then white Crane came flying down to the place where Frog was sitting and said, "I would like to try." He fastened his talons in the loops of Frog's harness, spread his great white wings and slowly, slowly lifted Frog into the air. When he was high above the marsh and the surrounding reeds, he headed toward Fire Mountain. To the people watching below, it seemed that he grew larger and larger, until he looked like a fleecy cloud with a blue misty lining.

But even the great, white Crane found that Frog was a much heavier load than he had expected, and he could not travel as fast as he wished. So he was forced to fly lower and lower, and, as he sailed over the top of the mountain, he thought he could hold Frog no longer.

"I must let go now! Anyway, we have reached one side of the mountain," he said to Frog. "And this is as far as I promised to carry you."

But Frog pleaded, "Oh! no! Do not let me fall now! I will shed a little water and then I will not be so heavy." So Frog shed one-fourth of the water he was carrying, and it fell on the mountainside in a torrent of black rain, quenching the fire on that side and afterward rising into the air as a thick, black mist.

Crane could then fly a little higher and he carried Frog across the mountain peak to the opposite side, where he said, "I must drop you now as I am getting very tired, and you are just as heavy as you were at first."

"Oh! no!" cried Frog, "I will make myself somewhat lighter and then you can carry me a little further." Again Frog shed one-fourth of the water he had brought from the swamp, and a heavy torrent of blue rain fell on that side of the mountain, quenching all of the fires and then rising in a thick, blue mist. After this Hosteen Frog was much lighter and Crane easily flew over the mountain to the eastern slopes. There Frog shed another fourth of his load, and white rain arose and soon turned into white mist. On the western side, Frog shed yellow rain from which a yellow mist arose. Now he had shed all of the water he had brought from the great marsh, and the fires had been quenched all around the mountain.

"We will go down and tell First Woman that the fires are out," said Frog. And Crane added, "Then we will go to our own homes in the marsh."

When the two stood in front of First Woman they said, "We have completed the task you set for us, and the fires have been quenched on all sides of the mountain. We used much water, and our swamp never will be as deep or as wide again. We ask you, in return for our labors, to refrain from taking water from our marsh henceforth, as it would soon be dry and we would have no place to live."

First Woman said, "We will take no more water from your swamp, and, furthermore, wherever the swamp water fell on the mountain sides, there will be small springs and marshy swales and these will belong to Crane and Frog."

She gave Crane charge of the white mists which hover over the ponds and lakes, and she gave Frog charge of the blue mists that rise from the marshes. Frog and Crane still live around the edges of the swamps among the reeds and water lilies. Crane is called a rainbird, and his feathers are used in the rain ceremonies. It is also said that the voice of Frog calls the rain, and if a person hears a frog crying "Har-ar-umph," he should try to catch him and tie him in the corn-field, to bring rain to the corn.

After the two had left for their homes in the marsh, First Woman looked toward Fire Mountain and was surprised to see mists of four colors hanging close above its peak. "What is this?" she asked.

And First Man answered, "That is the moisture that came from the swamp water when it fell on the fire. At first it was thin mist, but now it has gathered into clouds which hover above Fire Mountain and send down daily showers."

"That is a wonderful thing!" cried First Woman. "But those showers should not be in just one place! They should spread over the whole land!"

"That is the way it should be," agreed First Man. "Let us ask the Wind People to help us."

So messengers were sent to the four mountains of direction, where the Wind People lived in the highest caves. "The people need your help," the messengers told the four winds. "The First People wish you to blow the clouds in the four directions so rain may be distributed throughout the land." The four Wind People came from their caves and, with a loud, rushing noise, soon had clouds scattered everywhere across the sky, and showers were falling in many places.

Then First Woman said, "These clouds must have some place to stay when they are not traveling across the sky! They must have a home!"

The Wind People heard her words and answered, "When they have traveled over the whole land, we will take them to the mountains of the four directions to live with us. The black clouds will live on the northern peaks, the white clouds in the east, the blue in the south, and the yellow in the west." So that is the way the medicine men place cloud designs on their sandpaintings to this day.

Hosteen Crow giving First Woman four bundles of seeds he had brought
from the lower world

Chapter 14
SEEDS FOR THE FIFTH WORLD

WHEN ALL OF THE FIRST DINE'É
had decided on the proper method of building their homes,
they separated into clan families and journeyed to various locations to establish permanent dwellings. They chose sites
near springs or creeks of clear running water, and not too far
from mountain slopes where trees for firewood and for building purposes were to be found. As soon as each clan had selected an advantageous location and had built comfortable
homes, the people began to wonder about their food supply.
In the past they had moved from place to place gathering
seeds, nuts and berries wherever they were plentiful; when
the supply was exhausted they moved to another valley. But
now, because it would not be easy to move frequently, they
decided that they must have farms like the Pueblo Indians,
and raise their own food. Below them, in the fertile valleys,
they found level land that could be made into fine fields;

and they dug ditches to bring water from mountain streams so there could be moisture for the seeds. They divided the land into plots of equal size in order that each family would have its own field.

When this work was finished and the fields were ready to be planted, First Woman called a meeting and asked all who had fields to bring seeds for planting. She was especially anxious to have seeds of corn, beans, squash, melons and pumpkin. It was a large assembly as nearly all of the First People were present, and when they were seated in a wide circle First Woman asked, "Did someone bring corn, beans, squash, melons and pumpkin to plant in our fields?" No one answered her, and they all looked from one to another, thinking that surely someone had brought the seeds they needed. But it appeared that no one had.

"How is this?" she inquired. "The Stone House People have plenty of seeds of this kind, but the Dine'é have none!"

"It is because of Turkey," said First Man. "It was Turkey who brought all sorts of farm seeds from the lower world. When he was safe in this new land, he went to live with the Stone House People, and they now have wide fields of corn and beans, squash, melons and pumpkins, while we have not a single field."

"We must find out if anyone else brought seeds from the lower world," First Woman declared. "Perhaps Turkey was not the only one who thought to bring some, and perhaps other seeds will do just as well." Then she sent a messenger to Ant's house to ask if little Ant had brought any seeds from the lower world.

"Yes, I brought four kinds of seeds," Ant answered as she went into her storehouse and brought out four sacks filled with seeds. In one sack was grass seed, in the second was seed from the wild mustard, the third held seeds of the saltbush, while the fourth was filled with the tiny beans of the bee-weed. Now all of these plants would be useful to the Dine'é, and First Woman was glad to have the seeds. She thanked little Ant and gave her striped yellow jasper for her house. But these were not the seeds she had hoped to find; still they were better than none and would grow even when little rain fell and no other water was available for irrigating the fields where they were planted.

When the Dine'é saw the seeds little Ant had given them they said, "These seeds are small and do not look like much, but it is well that Ant brought them from the lower world, for we can use all of them. However, it does not seem likely they will produce enough food for us to live on during the long cold winter months."

First Woman said, "You are right! We will need more than this to harvest in the fall. I wonder who else may have brought a store of seeds?" Then she hurried to the home of Hosteen Squirrel who had his home in a hollow tree on the mountainside.

When she came to the tree, Squirrel was looking out of his door, so she said, "Hosteen Squirrel, did you bring any seeds from the lower world? We have cleared our fields and now we must have seeds with which to plant them."

Little Squirrel answered, "Yes! I brought four kinds of seeds to save them from the flood." Then he disappeared into the hollow tree which was his home, and came out carrying four sacks which he opened to show First Woman four varieties of seeds. In the first sack she saw piñon nuts, in the second were sweet acorns from the white oak, the third held pine cones, and the fourth held bur oak acorns.

"You have done very well to bring all these seeds from the lower world," said First Woman, "but they will all grow into trees, and we cannot have trees growing in our fields."

"Oh! no!" replied Squirrel. "These are for the mountain slopes, and I have already planted some far and wide, and now they are growing in many places to furnish nuts for the autumn harvest." First Woman thanked Hosteen Squirrel and gave him two black silk tassels to wear on the tips of his ears.

When First Woman told the people how Squirrel had planted oak, pine and piñon trees on the side of the mountain slopes, they said, "That is excellent! We can make good use of all of those things. We will roast the acorns and then grind the nut meats to make acorn flour. The oily piñon nuts can be crushed with grass seeds to make little cakes which we will bake on flat stones. Every fall, when the frost has opened the burs, we will go to the mountains to harvest acorns and nuts."

But First Man said, "We still do not have the seeds we need to plant in our fields!"

And First Woman said, "We will look a little further."

As they were walking along through the brush at the side of a creek, First Woman saw Mrs. Quail under a currant bush eating the ripe, red currants which had fallen to the ground. Her bill was stained red and red spots were on her vest. First Woman spoke to her and said, "We are walking about, looking for seeds to plant in our fields. Did you bring any seeds from the lower world?"

"Oh! Yes! I brought four kinds of seeds which I have planted along the banks of rills and creeks," replied speckled Quail.

"Which kind of seeds did you bring?" inquired First Woman.

"I brought berry seeds," Quail replied. "These I am eating are currants; and I also brought *Dzidzé,* the chokecherry, and raspberries and wild grapes. As long as these are ripe I have plenty to eat, and those that dry on the bushes furnish me with food throughout the winter. I planted the seeds when the mountains were first made, and now there are plenty of berries."

"Thank you, Mrs. Quail," First Woman said. "We, too, will gather the berries and dry them in the sun so they will last through the winter." Then she gave little Quail three white feathers to wear as a crest on her head.

When she told the others about the berry bushes Quail

165

had planted they said, "It will be nice to have berries with our seed cakes in the winter, but we still have no seeds with which to plant our farms!"

First Woman left the others standing by the bushes eating currants and raspberries, and walked away as she wished to make several more visits before darkness arrived. She hurried to the high rocks to find Hosteen Crow who had built his home in the crevice of a tall, smooth cliff. "Friend Crow," she said to him, "did you bring any seeds from the lower world?"

Hosteen Crow looked down to see who had spoken to him and espied First Woman standing at the foot of the rock. "Caw! Caw! Come up! Come up!" he called.

She looked one way and then another for a ladder or niches cut in the rock to form a stairway, but found neither. "I cannot climb the rock," she answered, "but I only want to know if you brought any seeds in your bundle when you came to this world!"

"Yes!" answered Hosteen Crow, "I brought the seeds of plants that had furnished me with food before the flood; I have four kinds." He disappeared into the crevice but soon came out with a carrying basket hung across his shoulders and held by a strap across his forehead. There were four divisions in this basket, and from one he took the seeds of the crow onion, and from the next seeds of the wild turnip. The third held seeds of white potatoes, and the fourth was filled with seeds from the wild parsnip. When Crow had given this basket of seeds to First Woman he said, "Plant these in your fields, water them, and see that the weeds do not hinder their growth. Then they will provide you with much food for your winter supply. Take them all! I have already planted all we shall need in the little meadows along the mountain sides, and soon there will be plenty for the Crow People." The basket was still filled with seeds, as it was Mother Earth's basket and would never be empty.

But First Woman said, "If you have planted these along

the mountain slopes, why should we plant them in our fields? We can come to the mountains and gather all we need without so much work."

Then Crow replied, "The potatoes, onions, turnips and parsnips that grow wild on the mountains will be small and hard, while those that grow in the fields will be large and sweet. You should not mind a little extra work!" Then First Woman thanked Hosteen Crow and gave him a sharp flint to wear on his beak. It is with this that Crow digs in the hard earth for the roots he gathers for his food.

When First Woman presented the basket to the people they said, "Certainly we are glad to have these things to add to our list of food, but even though we plant them in our fields they will fill only a small space, and we shall need more than this to last during the long cold months."

Now First Woman thought a long time before deciding where to go next. Finally she took the carrying basket and started for the home of little Duck who lived in the tall reeds at the edge of Muddy Lake. She stood beside the marsh where she saw Duck diving for polliwogs in the shallow water. "Little Duck," she called, "did you bring any seeds from the lower world?"

Little Duck swam toward the shore with her beak so full of moss and frog eggs that she could hardly speak. "Sack, sack! Sack, sack!" she said. And that is all she has been able to say from that day to this. When she understood First Woman's question, she went to her nest and brought out one sack filled with wild rice, another that contained wild millet, a third which held wild barley, and a fourth that was filled with the seeds of the sugar cane.

"These are the seeds I brought from the lower world," she informed First Woman. "This is the food I eat during the long, cold months of winter. I have planted them around all the marshy places I visit in the spring and in the autumn, so as to have food all along the way as I travel north or south."

"But will these grow when planted in our fields?" First Woman wanted to know.

"Water, water!" quacked little Duck as she turned toward the marsh.

"She means they will grow if we turn enough water onto the planted fields," First Man explained.

First Woman took the sacks of seeds saying, "These are the best of all!" Then, in return for the seeds, First Woman gave little Duck two curly feathers to wear in her tail, and little Duck is wearing those feathers to this very day.

First Man and First Woman hastened to the place where the Dine'é were waiting to show them the seeds little Duck had given them. When the people saw the contents of the four sacks, and then looked at the seeds and roots they had obtained from Crow and Ant, they said, "We are glad little Duck has given us these for we can make good use of them. Now we have many things to plant in our fields, and when our harvests are gathered and stored we will have food to last through the cold winter days."

The First People took all the seeds and roots and planted them in their fields, and they kept them well watered. They dug out all the weeds that tried to grow. In the autumn they had a good harvest, and all of the people worked night and day, gathering and storing the food until every storage pit and every storeroom was filled to overflowing.

For a time the Dine'é planted and harvested millet and barley, onions and potatoes, cane grass and turnips from their fields. Then later in the autumn, they moved to the mountains to gather acorns, pine cones and piñon nuts. It was slow, hard work as the seeds were small and it took many days of labor to fill even one sack. Even so, it was a great improvement over their previous manner of living. However, some of them went to visit their Pueblo neighbors and noted how plump and well-fed most of these people were, and how easy it was to harvest the corn, beans, squash and melons that grew in their fields. They also noticed that the Pueblo storerooms and storage pits were filled with food to last two or three winters. The Dine'é became dissatisfied with their own plants and the food they supplied; they began to wonder how they might obtain seeds to plant their fields with corn, beans, squash, melons and pumpkin.

"We will send someone to the Stone House People to ask for seeds," they said to each other. "Surely the rich Pueblo peoples will give us a few when they have more than they can use!"

Then First Woman looked around to find someone small and polite to send on this mission, and saw blue Lizard sunning himself on a rock. He was wearing a cream colored vest and a long coat that sparkled in the sun. First Women said, "I think Hosteen Lizard will be a good messenger to send to the People of the Stone Houses. He is clothed very neatly and he has a soft pleasant voice."

Now blue Lizard did not care to make the long journey to the south where the Stone House People had irrigated farms along the sides of the great river called Mother of Waters, so he said, "I cannot go for the seeds, as I have no basket or sack in which to carry them."

"I will make you a sack," offered Spider Woman. "I can make a sack that looks small when it is empty, but which will grow larger and larger to accommodate as many seeds as you wish to put in it."

"What will I take as a gift?" Lizard asked. "If I do not take them a gift, they will not admit me to their homes."

First Woman tried to think of something that would please the Stone House People, and finally decided to send a necklace of pink coral which she had brought from the lower world. This she hung around the neck of blue Lizard when he was ready to start on his journey.

Blue Lizard traveled toward the south all day and all night, reaching the homes of the stone house dwellers early in the morning. These people were just starting for their fields to gather the ripening corn when they saw Hosteen

Lizard approaching. "Who is this who comes so early in the morning, carrying an empty sack over his shoulders?" they asked each other. "It is only one of the Dine'é!" said someone. "And look what a queer necklace he is wearing! It is pink! I never knew that turquoise could be pink!" They said this because they thought all necklaces should be made of turquoise. No one had ever seen pink coral before.

Blue Lizard came near them and said, "I have brought you a beautiful necklace of pink coral to exchange for seeds from your fields. I would like to have the seeds of corn, beans, squash, pumpkins and melons to plant in our fields."

When the Stone House People heard this they laughed and said, "Who ever heard of wearing a necklace of pink coral! It is worthless, and no one would be seen wearing it! Now if you had brought a necklace of white shell beads, it would be of some value and we might give you farm seeds in exchange!" They seemed to consider this a great joke, and another person said, "We have no seeds to give to beggars! Go home and tell the Dine'é to be satisfied with roots and nuts!"

Little, blue Lizard hurried home to tell the First People how the Stone House People had laughed at him and refused the necklace. He handed the empty sack to Spider but he kept the coral necklace, which he still wears around his neck.

First Woman pondered for a minute and then said, "If it is white shell beads the Pueblo farmers want, then we must make white shell beads to exchange for their seeds. Will someone tell me where we can get the shell, and who can make these beads?" It was Crane who brought the white clam shells from the river bank; it was Ant who shaped them; and it was Locust who drilled the hole through the center. So, after a time, a double necklace of white shell beads was ready to be taken to the Stone House People.

First Woman tried to find blue Lizard but he had disappeared, so she said to Roadrunner, "Will you take this empty sack and this bead necklace to the south, where many

Stone House People live near the river called Father of Waters? They have irrigated fields and raise much farm produce. They will surely fill your sack when you give them this beautiful necklace!"

Now Roadrunner did not care to go on this long journey and said, "I cannot go on this errand for I have no way of carrying the sack when it is full of seeds."

"If you cannot carry the sack," First Woman replied, "we will give you a carrying basket." Then she asked Oriole for a basket she had made of grass and willow withes. Now this, too, was a magic basket, but unlike Spider's sack, it did not grow larger and larger as it was filled. Instead, the seeds in it grew smaller and smaller, so no matter how much was put into it the basket was never completely filled. It was fastened to Roadrunner's back and he started on his long journey toward the south.

He traveled all that night over dusty paths which led to the great river, and in the morning he came to a place where farmers were working in their fields. They saw Hosteen Roadrunner as he approached and said to each other, "Who is this who comes so early in the morning with an empty basket on his back?"

"Oh! That must be a messenger from the Dine'é who live far to the north," was the reply. "He looks dusty and tired and must have been walking all night!"

Another queried, "I wonder why he is making us a visit? What do you think he wants?"

Just then Roadrunner came up to them and said, "I have brought you a necklace of white shell beads to exchange for your farm seeds. We would like to plant corn, beans, melons and squash in our fields, but we do not have the seeds for planting."

The farmers took the necklace and examined it carefully, passing it from one person to another. "Yes, it is a nice necklace!" they all agreed. "But we cannot give you farm seeds until we hold a meeting, as these fields belong to the whole village." So a council meeting was held and Roadrunner waited outside the wall while the discussion was taking place, as he was not a member of their council. Everyone admired the necklace, but no one wished to part with a basket of seeds to pay for it. Finally one man spoke to the assembly and said, "I have one storage room that has been visited by mice and corn worms, so the seeds it contains are spoiled for planting. I will fill his basket with this useless seed and he will not know the difference, as the Dine'é know little about corn." So the Stone House People filled Hosteen's basket with wormy corn and took the white shell necklace as payment.

When Roadrunner arrived at the place where his friends were gathered they asked, "Did you get the seeds? Did you get the seeds?"

"Yes! I have all kinds of farm seeds. You may divide them as there will be enough for every field." Then he opened the basket and poured its contents on the ground where all the people could see.

First Woman looked at the corn and then picked up a handful to sniff the kernels. "This is not good corn!" she exclaimed. "It smells as though mice have been chewing it!"

Then they looked at the beans and someone said, "These beans are wormy, and the melon and squash seeds are wormy too! If we plant any of them, all our labor will be for nothing!" When Roadrunner heard this, he was so ashamed that he ran away and hid in the bushes but the Dine'é said, "It is not his fault. He thought he was bringing good, new seeds."

Now the First People did not know what to do. "We might send someone large and powerful to force the Stone House People to give us the seeds we need," a few suggested. Others advised raiding the fields and taking as much as they could carry. But no one really wanted to offend the stone house dwellers, so this suggestion was vetoed. After a while Hosteen Packrat came forward and said, "Let me try to get the farm seeds for you. I have a plan that may please everyone, even the Pueblo farmers."

They all looked at Packrat and wondered what his plan might be.

"I doubt if you can get the seeds," First Woman told him, "but it will do no harm to try, and anyway it will not be stealing for they have our white shell necklace and they surely owe us a basket of seeds for that!"

The other people shook their heads and said, "He will have no better luck than the others!"

Packrat paid no attention to all this talk, but slipped away to his home and looked at all the things he had hidden in his storeroom. All summer long he had been trading bright colored stones, feathers, bits of shell, and other objects for food that could be dried and eaten during the winter. Now he selected four large, red cactus apples and started for the stone houses in the east.

Late that night he arrived at a pueblo, and after a time found a crack in the storehouse wall large enough for him to enter. There he left the four cactus apples and took four bags of different colors of corn. The next morning when the Pueblos saw the four apples they said, "How nice these are! Someone has brought us this fine cactus fruit," and they never noticed that some of their corn was missing. The second night Packrat took four of the yucca bananas, that had grown on the great curved yucca to the south, to exchange for four kinds of beans, which he then hid in his storeroom. The third night he exchanged a basket of ground cherries for four varieties of vine fruit: melons, squash, pumpkins and gourds. Again the Stone House People were pleased with the presents he had left, and they did not miss the things he had taken. On the fourth night he left a sack filled with acorns and took four kinds of garden seeds: celery, beeweed, mustard and sunflower seed. And again the farmers were so pleased to have the acorns—as there were no oak trees in their country—that they failed to notice many seeds were missing.

Early in the morning of the fifth day, Hosteen Packrat called all of the First People together and asked them to come to his home. There he gave each family a share of the seeds he had brought from the villages of the Stone House People saying, "Now you have the same kind of seeds that are planted in the Pueblo fields; the people are still our friends; and no trouble has been caused." Packrat never told anyone how this peaceful exchange had been accomplished.

Hunter Boy shooting a cottontail rabbit with his bow and a stone-pointed arrow

Chapter 15

HUNTER BOY AND THE RABBITS

WHEN HOSTEEN PACKRAT made his trips to the stone houses of the Pueblos, he timed his journey so as to arrive at his destination just at sunset, when the Stone House People were preparing the food for their evening meal. He hid in the nearby rocks and saw the maidens grinding corn on stone *metates,* and the older women shelling pumpkin, squash and melon seeds to be ground with it. He watched a mixture being patted into round, flat cakes to be baked in conical adobe ovens in the patio. Now all this was not much different from the manner in which the Dine'é prepared their food. Although the First People had little corn to grind, they did have wild millet and grass seeds which they enriched with piñon nut meats and sunflower seeds. This mixture was pounded together with toasted yucca bananas to make small, flat, round cakes which were baked on

175

hot stones. But the Pueblos also prepared other food that Hosteen Packrat knew nothing about, and which smelled very good as it roasted slowly over an open fire. Being naturally curious, Packrat nosed around the bushes until he found where a deer had been dressed and cut into chunks for roasting and long strips for drying. Then he knew that the food roasting over the open fire was venison.

The First People had never eaten meat, as all of the animals who came with them from the lower world had been people like themselves and no game animals had been provided for their use. Therefore they had no weapons for hunting, and no traditions or ceremonial rites to guide them in this activity. When Packrat told the First People what he had seen, and explained how the Pueblos were roasting venison, they shook their heads and said that no one should ever think of killing animals for food. The animals would then become their enemies and there would be no peace in the world. But some of the younger men were interested and asked Packrat many questions.

One young man, who later was called Hunter Boy, asked about the bow and quiver of arrows, wanting to know what they were like and how they were used. He thought he would try to make some for himself, but the ones he made were so thick and clumsy they went only a little distance and then fell to the ground. When these proved of no use, Hunter Boy asked Packrat where the Pueblos kept their weapons.

"I saw them standing just outside the doorway," Packrat told him.

The next morning, long before the sun was up, Hunter Boy sent his pet crow to a stone house to steal a bow and quiver of arrows, if he could find them outside the door. It was not long until *Gáagi* returned with the hunter's bow and the quiver which held four feathered arrows, each with a sharp stone point. Hunter Boy took them and walked up the narrow canyon where he would be hidden from curious eyes, and there he practiced shooting at targets all day long. He became quite skilled at hitting the mark and, the next day, he started to walk around Huerfano Mountain in search of game. One of the arrows in the quiver was very beautiful, being made of red mountain mahogany, with three eagle feathers tied to the shaft and a black obsidian point at the tip. He made a little song to chant as he walked along.

As Hunter Boy walked swiftly toward the mountain, he saw a little cottontail rabbit sitting near a large bush. As the rabbit had never seen any of the Dine'é before, it was not afraid and sat quite still. Taking careful aim, Hunter Boy shot his best arrow and hit Rabbit. But his aim had not been true and the arrow only pierced the skin above Rabbit's shoulder. The frightened rabbit ran off with the arrow and dived into a hole under a large rock. Hunter Boy ran after him as fast as he could, and came to the rock just in time to see the rabbit disappear.

Tying his bow and quiver to his back, he started digging to make the rabbit hole larger, as he did not wish to lose his best arrow. He dug and dug, and sometimes he thought he could see the cottontail just a little ahead, but by the time he reached that spot the rabbit had gone. When he had tunneled several yards into the ground, he decided that he could go no farther and would have to give up his arrow and go back out of the tunnel. But when he tried to back out, he found that he had thrown so much loose dirt to his rear that the tunnel was filled and he could not get out. The hole he had made was so small that he could not turn around and he began wondering what he should do. Then he thought to himself, "That rabbit went somewhere! There may be another opening!" So he began digging off to one side, and suddenly he came to a little door of braided yucca which was much too small for him to enter.

As he was wondering what he should do a voice called to him, "Undo the thongs and come in!"

He answered, "The door is too small. I cannot get through!" Then the voice said, "Blow on it! Blow on it!"

Hunter Boy did as he was told, and immediately the little yucca door grew taller and wider until it was large enough for him to walk through. When he was through the door he looked around and found himself in a large underground room which was lighted very dimly by a thin shaft of light at one side. When he became accustomed to the dim light, he saw that this was the home of a large family of Rabbit People. There was grandfather rabbit, grandmother rabbit, mother and father rabbit and dozens of smaller rabbits. But these were not ordinary rabbits as their fur coats were now hanging on pegs around the walls and the Rabbit People looked just like the Dine'é. His arrow was lying on a bench near the opposite wall. The little rabbit he had shot was lying in front of the fireplace, wrapped in a fur robe.

Grandfather rabbit looked at Hunter Boy and said, "Take a seat on that pile of furs!" Then he asked, "Is that your arrow lying on the bench?"

Hunter Boy knew that it was his best arrow, for it was red with a black point, but he was afraid to claim it, so he said, "It looks like the one I had when I left home." And he began to wonder what would happen next.

But no one said anything more and they all continued with the tasks on which they had been working when he came into the room. Grandmother rabbit was mixing dough and making small biscuits about the size of peas. She dropped these into a pot of broth that was sitting near the fire, where they boiled and bubbled merrily. Near her was a small yellow bowl and when the stew was done, she took a wooden spoon and dished some into the bowl. "Bring me more bowls!" she commanded, and some rabbit girls brought her another and then another. And when these had been filled, the rabbit girls went into another room and brought her several more.

When all the bowls had been filled, grandmother rabbit handed the first one to grandfather rabbit to give to Hunter Boy. But grandfather rabbit refused to part with it, so grandmother filled another and handed it to him. After this she gave two bowls to the many children, one for the boys and one for the girls. The last one she kept for herself. Hunter Boy started eating from his bowl thinking that it held very little food for a whole meal, but fast as he ate, he could not diminish the amount of stew it contained, until he could eat no more; then suddenly the bowl was empty.

After they had eaten, grandfather rabbit looked sternly at Hunter Boy and asked, "How did you happen to come here?"

Hunter Boy hardly knew what to say. He did not wish the Rabbit People to know that he had stolen the bow and arrows from the Stone House People, and this was the first hunting trip he had ever taken, so he said, "I saw something hopping in the bushes and shot my best arrow at it. When it ran away, I followed to get my arrow."

"Did you know that you had injured my grandson?" grandfather rabbit wanted to know.

"No, I hardly knew what it was that had been hit, because it disappeared under the rock."

Grandma rabbit said to all the little rabbits, "Go out, my dears, and gather seeds for tomorrow's food, for I have used all that we had in the storeroom."

So they put on their fur coats, took the yellow bowls in their hands and went out of the room. As they went, grandma rabbit warned them, "Be sure to hide well under the weeds and bushes for Hosteen Coyote and grandfather Owl will be looking for you if you stray out where you can be seen!"

It was not long until they all came back with their bowls full of seeds.

"Are any missing?" their grandmother asked.

"We are all here," was the reply.

"Take off your coats and start mashing the seeds with the stone pestle," she directed. Soon they were all busy pounding the seeds into mush.

Grandfather rabbit stood up and spread his fur robe on the floor. "Go bring the other things," he said to the boy rabbits.

A dozen rabbit boys went into another room and brought out many armloads of cattails that had been clipped from the bulrushes near the lake. These they heaped in the center of the fur robe, so they made a large pile. Grandfather rabbit then grasped the corners of the robe and swung it over his shoulder. Now he spoke to Hunter Boy. "Come, my friend, it is time for us to go."

The two left the rabbits' home and walked to the top of a high butte that stood alone on the wide plain. Here Rabbit Man opened the bundle and threw one-fourth of the cattails to the east, another fourth to the south, the next to the west, and the last to the north. Then he blew toward the four directions and immediately the brown cattails turned into rabbits which hopped away into the bushes. When he had folded the empty robe and tucked it under his arm, he turned to Hunter Boy and said, "I have created these rabbits so that you may have game to hunt and meat to eat. Kill as many as you need for food, but do not kill wantonly or they will disappear. Do not eat the meat without cooking it well, and never eat either the liver or the heart, or you will become ill and die." Then he disappeared behind the butte and Hunter Boy did not see him again.

Running down the east side of the butte, Hunter Boy took an arrow from his quiver and shot a rabbit. Picking up the rabbit and the arrow, he circled to the south side of the rock and shot another, and then one of the western side and another on the north. Tying their hind legs together, he threw them over his shoulders, as they were heavy and he had a long way to travel to reach his home. He walked all the remainder of the day and hid in a tangle of cacti during the hours of darkness, as he was afraid someone would follow the scent of the game he was carrying.

It was midday when he arrived at the home of First Woman to give her the rabbits and to tell the story of his encounter with grandfather rabbit. He also told her how the rabbits he had been permitted to kill were created so the

Dine'é could add meat to their list of foods. Then he repeated the warning grandfather rabbit had given him. "The meat must be well cooked, and no one must ever eat the liver or the heart!"

First Woman had lived with the Stone House People and was the only one who knew how meat should be prepared and cooked for food. Calling all of the people together, she showed them how to dress the rabbits and how to stuff them with sage and bits of saltbush. Then she said, "As these game animals have their homes underground, it is best that they be cooked underground."

First Man and his helpers moved the fire and coals from the firepit and dug a shallow place in the ground to serve as an oven. First, the four rabbits were well wrapped in sage and saltbush leaves, and then in mustard leaves and long blades of peppergrass. The oven was lined with watercress and then the rabbits were placed inside. After the ashes and coals were raked over the top, a good fire was built and kept burning for several hours.

In the late afternoon all of the First People assembled to await the opening of the oven. First Man scraped away the fire and the ashes, then many helpers with sharp oak sticks removed the rabbits from the oven. When the charred leaves and twigs had been peeled away, the meat was found to be well cooked and wonderfully flavored. The four rabbits were divided so that everyone could have a portion, and they all declared it to be the best food they had ever tasted.

Hunter Boy was greatly praised for his efforts in securing this game, and was unanimously appointed chief hunter, or Hunt Chief, for all the First People.

Deer Farmer in the guise of a deer; and Hunter Boy as a small white dog

Chapter 16

HUNTER BOY AND THE DEER

HUNTER BOY DECIDED TO VEN-
ture forth on another hunting trip. He went toward the
western mountains called the Carrizos. After hunting all
morning he had four large rabbits hung on his shoulder
strap. Suddenly he came to a long brush house.

There he saw several people who had come from Pueblo
villages far to the west, to hunt for meat. These people, Hosteen Puma, Wolf, Lynx and Coyote, were hunters that had
been sent out by their clans when it was reported that many
rabbits had been seen on this side of the mountain. These
hunters had built the brush lodge to use as their camp during
their stay in the area.

The hunters, each of whom came from a different pueblo,
had brought two Bird People with them—Hosteen Magpie
and his wife. Hosteen Magpie flew ahead of the hunters to

locate the game. When it had been sighted, Hosteen Coyote ran widely around the game and drove it to the place where the hunters were hidden. None of the hunters had bows and arrows; they depended on long clubs when the game was near, or on curved sticks when it was some distance away. These sticks, somewhat like boomerangs, were called rabbit sticks. The hunters had been seeking game for three days but nothing had been killed.

Puma said to the boy hunter, "Where did you get your rabbits?" And Wolf said, "We have hunted for three days and have not seen even one, while you have killed four in one morning!"

Then the boy gave the hunters three of his rabbits, which they were glad to get, for they were very hungry. Quickly they skinned and dressed them, laid them out on flat stones and started pounding the meat, fat and bones all together until it was like mush; then they ate it. The white stones with which they did the pounding were "star stones" that cooked the meat as it was being crushed.

When all had eaten, and the little white dog that belonged to Hosteen Puma had been fed, Wolf again asked Hunter Boy, "Where did you get your rabbits?"

Hunter Boy replied, "I was given rabbits for game for the Dine'é. I have been inside the home of the Rabbit People."

They all asked, "Where is it? Where is it?"

When he told them, they all started for the rabbits' house, but when they arrived at the big rock, the hole underneath was much too small for any of them to crawl through. That rock is called *Gah Bék'izí* to this very day.

The boy went with the hunters all that afternoon; although Coyote and Lynx saw many rabbits, they did not succeed in killing one. Hunter Boy killed six and gave them to the six hunters so they returned to the brush house well pleased.

During the entire time of the hunting trip, as they traveled from one place to another through valleys and over hills and mesas, Hunter Boy killed rabbits for their food supply, being careful to kill only enough to satisfy their hunger.

The other hunters brought back nothing as they were looking for deer, and there were no deer. They started to hunt in the mountains and traveled until they came to two high peaks near Crystal Springs, where they left their white star stones. That place is now known as *So Silá*, or Star Mountain, and below the crest is *Tótligai,* or White Water Lake. There they were joined by other hunters who had been walking the game trails for four days but had found nothing. Now they were faint with hunger. Hunter Boy killed a large number of rabbits so everyone was fed.

All this time, while Coyote was scouting all the trails, the two magpie scouts had been flying around the cliffs and the mountaintop. The next morning Coyote said, "Somewhere there are plenty of deer, and Deer Farmer knows where they are!" Coyote had seen Deer Farmer's house when he was going across the mountain, and had noticed a deer pelt hanging over the door.

Now Deer Farmer was not a Navaho, nor was he a Pueblo. His ancestors were the *Yé'ii,* who had lived in the cliff houses for generations and were now few in number, and these few were not friendly toward newcomers. It was said that Deer Farmer was a great magician who could change himself into a coyote, or a snake, or a deer if he so wished. He was in charge of all the deer, antelope, elk, mountain sheep, and other game animals that lived on this mountain. When the new people arrived he had herded them into a wide, deep crater on the mountaintop. Here was plenty of water and grass for grazing, so the animals were well fed and content to remain. Only one narrow canyon led through the rocks to this meadow, and Deer Farmer had built a wall across it. He left a narrow doorway which he blocked with a large slab of rock, so wide and heavy that no man was strong enough to move it. Deer Farmer had a magic cane made of turquoise and flint with which he opened the door. Only the cliff people knew what had become of the deer, and they were the only ones who had meat to eat whenever they desired.

Coyote, who was a sly fellow, said to Hunter Boy, "I have a plan by which we can find out where the deer are hidden!" The hunters were anxious to know what this plan could be, and Coyote said, "The little white dog can manage to get into Deer Farmers' home. Hunter Boy must borrow the dog's white coat and stay at Deer Farmer's house until he learns the secret hiding place."

Cougar and the other hunters did not like this plan very well, but they could suggest nothing better, and Lynx said, "This plan may fail, but it is worth trying."

So Hunter Boy put on the dogskin coat and became as small as the little dog, and Wolf said, "He looks like a dog, but he must not try to bark." The boy's pet crow had followed him on this hunting trip and he now grasped Hunting Boy in his claws and flew away toward the mountains. He had been told to do this by Coyote who directed him to the place where Deer Farmer lived with his wife and one daughter.

The hunters who were at the brush lodge watched the crow as it flew round and round from one peak to another and finally went to Rainbow Bridge, not far from Chinle. There the crow flew through the hole under the rock four times, with the white dog still in his claws. They could barely see him as he was a long distance away, but just as the sun was setting, they saw him light on Blue Peak. Then the hunters were worried and said, "Where is our friend now? Where did the crow go with the one who has fed us on this long trip?"

The magpie, who was able to see a long distance, and occupied the position of watcher, said, "He flew to the home of Deer Farmer to learn where the deer are hidden."

Now when the crow arrived at the home of Deer Farmer he flew low and dropped the little dog just outside the door. As soon as the crow had disappeared, the dog began to whine and scratch at the door in order to gain admittance. Deer Farmer's daughter was in the house and asked, "What can this be? It must be something the crows have brought to our door," and her father and mother asked the same question.

When the door was opened, they saw the little dog on the doorstep and felt sorry for him, as it was dark and cold outside the house. The daughter begged her father to let her take it into the house and keep it for a pet. He did not refuse her request, and she took it in and held it in her lap, stroking its white coat. But her father did not approve of this. Then the girl requested her mother to make a bowl of cornmeal mush so the little dog could have something to eat. But when it was offered to him, the dog refused to eat any of it. Deer Farmer put a stick in the fire and held it there until one end was red-hot. He would have burned the dog's eyes with it, but his daughter would not allow him to do so. That evening the girl made a soft bed of deer hair upon which the dog could sleep. But the thick coat Hunter Boy was wearing smothered him and he was too warm in the house. Besides, he was certain that Deer Farmer would attempt to kill him as soon as the others were asleep. He asked permission to sleep on the flat roof and went up there, where he could watch for his pet crow to come in the early morning.

The next morning the girl said, "I wonder what this strange dog will eat?" And when he came inside the room, she stripped bits of fat from the deer meat they were eating and this was his breakfast. Then she said, "Look, Father! He likes deer meat. He has eaten all that I gave him!" And that day he was given all the meat in the house. Again he slept on the roof, and when the girl opened the door in the morning to give him a bowl of porridge, he refused to eat it.

Then the girl said to her father, "Father, we must get some fresh meat for the dog. That is all he will eat."

The father answered, "If your dog will not eat corn mush or corncakes, let him starve!"

But the girl was afraid her pet would die without fresh meat, and she kept coaxing her father to bring home a deer. Finally Deer Farmer agreed to bring venison home for them if they would all stay there and wait for him, but the daughter said, "No! We will all go with you for the venison!"

The family prepared for their visit to the deer meadow by painting themselves white and wearing grey deer hide robes over their shoulders. Deer Farmer wore a hood with deer horns on his head, and even the little dog was covered with deer hair, to make them look like a group of animals walking through the bushes.

As they went along they came to a place where two blue-birds waited to give warning of danger, but Deer Farmer waved his wand at the birds and they remained silent. A little farther on they came to an old tree on which sat two red-headed woodpeckers that started drumming on the tree, to send forth a warning. Deer Farmer commanded them to be silent and the party went past safely. Soon they came to two white-headed woodpeckers and then two humming birds who allowed them to pass. When these guards had been left behind, they came to the mouth of a narrow canyon which they entered, and walked between high, rocky walls. After a time they came to the large slab of rock which closed the entrance to the deer meadow. Deer Farmer struck the slab four times with his turquoise wand and the rock slid away, leaving the door open.

Deer Farmer called to the deer in a shrill voice, "Ohie! Ohie!" which was his call to them. When he had given this call four times, a deer came to the door. He took it by the horns and pulled it out through the opening. As soon as it was well away from the door, Deer Farmer struck the slab with his wand and again it slid over the opening. Deer Woman covered it with brush so no one would notice that it had been moved. The dog watched all of this very carefully. He now had found where the deer were hidden and how it might be possible for his friends to obtain game.

After going a short distance, Deer Farmer killed the deer and cut up its flesh for meat, but he did not harm the head, the bones, or the entrails. He placed these on the deerhide in the same order they had been when the deer was alive, and folded the hide around them so the deer could return to life. When they were at home once more, the daughter gave the little dog all the fat meat he could eat. Deer Farmer and his wife were not pleased to see this strange dog eating all the best of the meat. They would have killed him, only they were afraid of offending their daughter who was a grown woman now, and, as they had no other children, they were afraid she might leave home.

All this time the little dog refused to sleep inside the house, but curled up near the smokehole in the roof. Every night, just before dawn, his pet crow came to talk to him, advising him to not stay in this place too long, as these people were his enemies.

Every morning the girl took him into the house and fed him the choicest bits of fat venison.

"Why do you not make him sleep inside?" the father asked his daughter.

"No, Father!" the girl replied. "It is too hot in here and he might suffocate!"

So the dog slept on the roof near the smokehole throughout the night, and Deer Farmer placed the fur robes on which he slept underneath the opening, so he could watch the dog. As long as Deer Farmer was watching, Hunter Boy did not dare to leave the roof. When his pet crow, who was perched on the edge of the roof, asked him why he did not leave, now that he knew where the deer were hidden, Hunter Boy replied, "I cannot leave as long as Deer Farmer is awake. He would follow and try to kill me!"

"I think I can do something about that!" exclaimed the crow and flew away toward the south.

Near morning, Hunter Boy heard the sound of someone flying toward the roof and looked up to see a whippoorwill coming from the rice marsh. Down through the smokehole he flew, then round and round beneath the ceiling, shaking marsh dust from his feathers over the sleeping family. This heavy pollen was an opiate which brought instant slumber to anyone who breathed it, and Deer Farmer immediately fell into a sound sleep. Then the whippoorwill flew out of the house and said to the little dog, "You can go now! They are all fast asleep!"

Hunter Boy removed his dogskin coat and, tucking it under his arm, he scrambled down the side of the house, making a scratching noise. Deer Farmer's wife, who had been sleeping with her robe pulled over her face, had not breathed the marsh pollen, and she heard the scratching noise. Going to the old man, she pulled the robe off his shoulders and shook him saying, "Wake up! Wake up! Go outside and see what is climbing down the wall, making a scratching noise!" But Deer Farmer did not waken.

Hunter Boy started for the place where the deer were penned and ran rapidly up the canyon until he came to the rock gate. Looking around in the bushes, he found the turquoise wand that had been hidden there by Deer Farmer. Then, standing in front of the large slab of rock, he hit it four times saying, "Open! open!" at each blow. Slowly, the huge slab slid to one side exposing the wide doorway, through which Hunter Boy stepped.

He looked across a beautiful meadow where many varieties of game animals were grazing. Remembering the words Deer Farmer had used to call the deer, he shouted, "Ohie! Ohie!" and when a large flock of animals gathered in front of him he said, "Wah-ohie! Wah-ohie!" Then he stepped aside and allowed all the male deer to run through the opening. When they were gone, he cried "Bah-ohie! Bah-ohie!" and all the does ran out. After this he called "Mah-ohie! Mah-ohie!" and all the young deer passed through the gate. He did not close the opening but shouted, "Yah-ohie!" to all the other game animals in the meadow to let them know they could leave if they wished to be free. A great many elk, antelope, mountain sheep, and jack rabbits came through the opening; the goats were the only ones that remained in the meadow. Hunter Boy did not try to kill any of these game animals as he had no bow or arrows, and he was still carrying the white, dogskin coat. He told the freed animals that the mountains, hillsides, and valleys would now be their homes, and they were free to graze where the grass was the greenest and the water the sweetest. From that time many deer have lived on the mountains, furnishing game for the people who depend on hunting to obtain food.

When Deer Farmer finally awoke, he and his wife ran toward the canyon as fast as they could; as it was not yet daylight they stumbled and fell over rocks and bushes, and their progress was slow. When they arrived at the gate they found it open, and many animals were still escaping. Deer Farmer snatched up the turquoise wand lying beside the path. He hit the stone with it four times, and closed the door. Then he broke the wand into small pieces and tossed them over the top of the rock gate so they landed in the bushes on the other side. "Now!" he declared, "It will not be possible for any mortal to open this door again."

Deer Farmer upbraided his daughter bitterly saying, "See now what you have done! It is you who have caused us all this loss! We were the only ones who had venison, and robes, and buckskins with which to make our clothing! Now my deer are scattered everywhere!"

The mother was sorry for her daughter when she heard these angry words. She said to Deer Farmer, "Why do you scold so loudly? There is no way to change this thing that has happened! Are you not as well able to hunt through these mountains as the Earth People?" And so the old man said no more.

As the deer were escaping through the gateway, Hunter Boy's pet crow flew down and perched on a rock. "You must leave here at once!" he said. "Deer Farmer and his wife are coming, and if they find you here they will kill you."

Hunter Boy was still carrying the dogskin coat under his arm, and now he started putting it on. As he pulled it over his head he grew smaller and smaller, and when it came down to his feet he had shrunk in size until it was just a snug fit. "Now carry me back to my friends at the camp!" he commanded the crow.

The crow picked up the little dog in his claws and flew away toward the east. When he came to the Rainbow Bridge he again flew under it four times, being careful to fly in the direction opposite to his first flight. Then he flew from peak to peak, opposite to the direction he had taken at the start of his journey, and soon he came within sight of the brush house.

Mrs. Magpie was keeping watch at the hunters' camp, and as she looked toward the west she saw a dark speck in the sky; she said to her husband, "Fly quickly along all the trails and tell the hunters to return to camp, for crow is coming with Hunter Boy." So Hosteen Magpie spread the word, and all of the hunters were waiting when the two arrived. Hunter Boy handed the white coat to its rightful owner and picked up his own robe. Then he spoke to his friends: "I went to the home of Deer Farmer near the top of a high mountain. It has been a long journey, and it was a dangerous task to find the deer and to set them free. But I opened the gate at the top of the mountain, and many escaped. Now game will be provided for all hunters."

Hunter Boy never went back into the canyon where the animals had been trapped. He had accomplished his mission, and many of the game animals had been given their freedom.

That is how it came about that deer, antelope, and occasionally larger game, such as elk and mountain sheep, have been in the land of the Dine'é. The animals lived and increased in numbers until plenty of game was available for all of the hunting peoples. This game provided meat to eat, robes, and buckskin for making garments, sinew for their bows and for sewing, deer bone needles, awls, and other implements. To the Indians of the mountains, the deer furnished as much in the way of food, clothing, and useful tools as did the bison to the Indians of the plains.

A round house of log walls and earth-covered domed roof, with doorway
in the east, came to be the Navaho home, or *hogan*

Chapter 17

HOMES FOR THE DINE'É

During the first years of
their life in the Fifth World, while the mountains and the
rivers were being created to resemble those which had been
left behind, the First People had made their homes near
rivers or springs, or near the Place of Emergence which had
become a wide lake. But, after the clouds were formed and
rain came splashing down to make rills, springs and lakes on
the mountains and in the valleys, it was no longer necessary
to remain grouped in two or three places. Water was everywhere, and one could wander far and wide to gather the seeds,
nuts and berries on which they lived. Until now they had

been content to return each night to the crowded caves, dug-outs or brush shelters that served as their homes, where they could shut out the bleakness of the hostile land during the hours of darkness.

After the coming of the rains, the valleys and mesas were green with grasses and bright with flowering shrubs, while trees grew beside the streams and on the mountain slopes. No longer was it necessary for the people to remain in these crowded shelters which were filled with smoke in the winter and dust in the summer. Besides, food was becoming increasingly scarce in the vicinity of their dwellings. Of course some were content to remain in these poor homes, but many others said, "Let us find sheltered places near the hills or at the foot of some mountain and build ourselves homes that will be warm in winter and cool when summer heat arrives." Others said, "We should not live in a place that has become barren because too many people are living near."

So the Dine'é began to divide into family and clan groups, and to move to different places. One of the vexing problems was the division of household property which had been considered a communal resource up to that time. When a fair distribution had been arranged to the satisfaction of the older people, their things were packed and they made ready for journeying in different directions to establish new homes.

While they were still grouped together First Woman spoke to the people, saying, "It is now possible to build houses of any size or shape you may desire, and to use whatever materials are most convenient. Tall trees will furnish logs; square stones occur along the canyon walls; and firm adobe, or clay, is available from which bricks may be made. But before you start building, it might be wise to consult the people who were among the first to construct homes in this new world and who have lived in them long enough to know their advantages and their shortcomings."

Now, it seems that the Bird People, who had been the first through the emergence passage, were also the first to find material for building their homes in safe places. So First Woman spoke to them and asked, "Can anyone show us how to make a warm house that will be a protection at night, and which the strong winds will not blow away, or the hard rains and hail destroy?"

"I will show you how I built my home," screamed grey Eagle as he flew to a rock crevice roofed by an overhanging ledge, high on the crest of Blue Mountain. They all watched as Eagle carried sticks and short poles to build a hollow circle twice his own height, which he lined with twigs from the spruce trees and feathers from his own breast. "This is the way to build a house," he told the First People. "My children will be safe inside these stout walls, and neither wind nor rain can reach them." This was certainly a good, safe place in which to live, but it was much too high for those who could not fly.

First Woman examined this house carefully and then said to Eagle, "We are glad to see how your house is built and we, too, will go into the high mountains in the summer time and will build cool shelters of poles and brush. But this will not be warm enough for the cold winter months."

Eagle said, "We fly far away during the winter, but always return to this home early in the spring."

First Woman who was still looking at Eagle's nest said, "You have shown us how to put the poles together to form a circle. We will follow this plan so that our houses will be round like the sun." She thanked Eagle and gave him white shell beads to wear on his headdress.

As they walked away from this mountain they heard another bird's voice saying, "Come with me and I will show you how to build a very warm house which the winds cannot blow away or the rains enter."

It was Mrs. Oriole who spoke these words. They followed her as she led the way to a tall cottonwood tree that stood near a rambling creek in which willows and tall marsh grasses were growing. High in the treetop she chose a stout branch that would not break in a storm, and then brought long strips of willow bark and leaves of marsh grass which she wove together to make a snug basket with an opening at one side. When this nest was solid, she lined it with fuzz from the milkweed pods and the cliff rose. Then she said, "Look at my home! It is high enough to be out of danger from snakes or skunks who would like to steal my eggs, and it is protected from the rain and the sun by the branches above it." The First People said, "Yes! it is a beautiful nest but we cannot live in the top of a tree." So they left Mrs. Oriole in her home and walked away. But First Woman stayed to thank Oriole, and said, "It is true that we cannot build our houses in the tree tops, but you have taught us some very useful lessons. From now on we will weave the baskets, which we use for gathering seeds and nuts, in the manner you have taught us. We will make our large carrying baskets from strong willow withes and marsh grasses, and we will also make ropes to fasten them across our shoulders." Then she gave Oriole yellow beads for her throat decoration.

As they turned away from the cottonwood tree, Hosteen Woodpecker flew in front of them. "Come with me!" he cried, "come with me and I will show you the easiest way to build your homes!" He led the people to a river valley where a tall hollow tree stood. He clung to the bark on the east side and started pecking a hole in the side of the trunk, to use as a door. "Rap-rap, rap-a-rap-tap," was a hollow noise that could be heard for a long distance. After a time the hole was large enough for him to enter and he disappeared inside the tree. As they waited he stepped out again and said, "There is plenty of room in here and, when I have brought grasses and soft moss, it will be a pleasant place in which to live."

But First Woman shook her head. "It certainly will be a nice, safe place for you and your family," she told him, "but the Dine'é cannot live in hollow trees. However, you must not be disappointed, for you have given us a useful gift. We have heard the sound of a drum and now we will use this sound to call our people to council meetings, and to summon help in time of emergencies." Then she thanked Woodpecker and gave him red beads to wear in his headdress.

When Cliff Swallow saw that the First People were still looking for the correct method of home building he said, "Come with me! I have made a strong warm house! Come with me and I will show you how it was done." Quickly he flew to an overhanging cliff and selected a curved place on the under side. He then flew to a little pond with adobe banks and filled his claws with chunks of adobe. This he mixed with bits of grass and built walls that clung to the solid rock. This mud house was round, with a door at the side, and was protected from sun, rain and all enemies by the overhanging cliff. As the First People looked at it they said to each other, "This seems to be a very solid house which the wind cannot blow away and the rain cannot reach." But others shook their heads and said, "It is too high in the cliffs for us. We would need ladders to reach such a high place." And some said, "There would be no place to store our winter supply of seeds and nuts." So the people turned to go away, but First Woman said, "Thank you, Cliff Swallow, for showing us how to make plaster of adobe, dry grass and water, which will be of great use to us in covering our walls and making hard, smooth floors." Then she gave Swallow some black jet beads to decorate his coat and turned away.

A few of the people stayed at the cliffs and searched for a path to climb the steep rock wall. "This place suits us very well," they said, "and this is where we will build our homes. There are plenty of rocks with which to make the walls, and adobe for plaster to hold them together." Then they examined the cliffs until they found a wide ledge of flat rock that would serve as a floor, while an arched projection made a natural roof. It was a wonderful location for a home if they did not mind climbing down the steep side of the canyon every time they stepped out the front door. These people built long rows of rooms in caves and soon became known as the "Cliff House People," or the Cliff Dwellers.

When the remainder of the people turned away from the cliffs, they were most discouraged and said, "We have visited the homes of the Bird People and have not found a house to our liking. Now where shall we go?" But First Woman reproved them saying, "Do not be impatient! It is true that we have spent much time visiting houses that we could not use, but in doing so we have learned many important things. We have learned from Eagle how to lay logs to form circular walls, from Oriole how to plait grass and reeds into baskets; from Woodpecker we have learned how to send messages to distant places, and from Swallow, how to plaster our homes with adobe. I think this is all we can learn from the Bird People, so let us now visit the homes of our four-footed friends." Many of the people objected to this suggestion saying, "The homes of Bear, Wolf, Fox and Coyote are just caves in the hillsides or in the jumbled rocks on the mountains. We have occupied caves and rock shelters long enough. We wish to build homes that are larger and better than any we have had." They all agreed that the mountain animals would be of little help with this problem.

"Perhaps we can learn something from the Water People," First Woman suggested. The others looked doubtful but agreed to journey along the river bank and talk to whomsoever they found living there. The first person they encountered was Hosteen Muskrat whose home was in a tangle of roots and brush completely surrounded by shallow water and marsh grass. Its entrance was underwater, and its inhabitants would need to be good swimmers to live there. Although this looked like a good, safe place to build a home, the First People left the home of Muskrat and went to call on Hosteen Mink and Hosteen Otter who had built their homes in tangled thickets of brush and logs that filled a swampy cove near the river. "This will never do for us!" the First People decided. "It is dark and damp under those logs, and besides, it smells of fish!"

So they moved farther down the river to a long dam of brush and mud that held water in a large pond. The Beaver People had built this dam to raise the water of the pond high enough to guard their houses. Everyone looked at the dome-shaped roofs they could see just above the water, and noticed how they were built in beehive fashion, with an opening at one side for ventilation. The walls of these houses were also built of crossed logs and were two stories high. The lower rooms were underwater and the doorway led through these to the upper rooms which were above water and comfortably dry. "These are wonderful houses!" First Woman exclaimed. "They are large and well built. Fresh air and sunlight can enter through the openings in the roof and the underwater entrance can be closed with reeds." Then she asked the Beaver People to show the Dine'é how to lay the short poles to form the beehive roof. "We will not build our homes in the water," she announced, "but we can copy this good solid roof wherever we may build." Then she thanked the beavers and gave them an abalone shell.

As they turned away from the river and walked toward the mesa, they saw a cottonwood tree several branches of which were covered with a silk net. "What is that?" they asked, and First Woman said, "That is the home of Mrs. Caterpillar. Let us see what she can tell us about building a house." This house seemed to be a large ball of silk net that was fastened over the leafy ends of many twigs. The rooms and passageways were filled with dozens of small caterpillars, some of which were moving from room to room while others were busily eating the green leaves. Mrs. Caterpillar was standing in her doorway watching the approach of the First People.

When they were near First Woman said, "You have a very fine house here in the cottonwood tree! Would you kindly explain to us how you built it?"

Mrs. Caterpillar stretched herself along a bare cotton-wood twig and then replied, "I wove it from silk threads that had been wound around my body. I covered as many green leaves as I could so my large family would have food."

"It looks so thin," First Woman marveled, "will not the wind and the rain spoil it?"

"Sometimes that happens," Mrs. Caterpillar replied, yawning, "but it really is quite strong, and I can always mend it."

"How do you keep the birds from eating all your children?" First Woman wanted to know.

"Oh! I am not bothered by the birds," Mrs. Caterpillar stated. "You see, this tent is tough and sticky, so if the small birds who hunt for worms fly into it their wings are covered with the net and they cannot fly. Sometimes silly birds try to come through the doorway, then their heads are covered with the inner net and they are almost blinded. They do not come back."

"These walls seem very thin for the cold days of winter," First Woman remarked.

"Oh! we do not remain here during the cold winter," replied Mrs. Caterpillar. "By that time my children are old enough to bore holes in the bark of trees and are snugly protected, while I rewrap the silken threads around my body to form a warm cocoon where I sleep until summer comes again.

"This tent house is all very well for you, but it would be of little use to us. We have no silk with which to make tents and have no wish to live under the bark of cottonwood trees!"

So the First People journeyed on, still looking for the kind of home that would suit their needs.

The next home they visited was that of Spider Woman who was in the meadow, busily spinning a fly trap from one daisy to another, when she saw the group approaching. Quickly she ran to a hole in the ground that was her doorway, climbed down the swinging ladder and pulled a blanket over the opening.

"Who was that running away from us?" asked First Woman.

"That was Spider Woman, and she must have her home underground for she disappeared through that hole," replied First Man.

So First Woman walked to the opening and called, "Mrs. Spider, are you there?"

And Spider replied, "Come in! Come in! We are waiting for you!"

First Woman looked at the opening and said, "The hole is much too small, we cannot get through."

The voice of Spider Woman advised, "Try it! Try it!"

So First Woman put one foot into the opening, which immediately became large enough for the other foot and then for her whole body. Backing down the passage, she came to the ladder which she thought too small and frail to carry her weight.

"Climb down! Climb down!" commanded a shrill voice.

First Woman started climbing cautiously down the ladder, step by step, but was only halfway down when it began to swing wildly from side to side so she could hardly cling to it. Soon it began to whirl one way and then turn and whirl the other way. Hosteen Spider was doing this by means of a long rope tied to the bottom of the ladder. When First Woman became dizzy and fell to the floor, the spider family rolled their eyes and laughed, showing their sharp, ugly teeth.

As First Man was descending the ladder, Hosteen Spider treated him the same way so he, too, fell to the floor, as did the next two who tried to enter. First Man was angry and said, "Why do you treat us so unkindly? We have done you no harm!"

To which Spider replied, "It is a game we play with all who enter. We find it quite amusing." And then he asked, "Why do you come into our home when you are not invited?"

First Woman answered, "We came to see if you could tell us how to build a house that would be cool in summer but warm in winter."

"You have come to the right place," Hosteen Spider said. "This house answers those qualifications, and it was easy to build." He looked around the room at his wife and their many children. "We followed a root that grew deep in the ground, and when we came to softer earth we carried it away, bit by bit, until we had a room large enough for our family to be comfortable.

First Woman saw that the room was large and was divided into four parts by blankets hanging from the ceiling. "Where did you get all those fine blankets?" she inquired.

"I made them myself," answered Spider Woman, "I am a very good weaver." Then she showed First Woman a loom standing against the south wall. "Hosteen Spider brought the poles and reeds to build the loom," she stated, "so I weave while he twists the ropes into ladders or nets."

"These are things we could use," declared First Woman. "Will you teach me to weave?"

"You cannot weave until you have thread or yarn," stated Mrs. Spider. "When you have these, come back and I will teach you."

So the First People left the home of the spiders, promising to return in order to learn how to weave and how to braid ropes and nets for catching small game. As she left, First Woman thanked the spiders and gave them a shell filled with red berries saying, "These berries can be used to dye the threads you use in your weaving, so you can make beautiful patterns in your blankets."

After this they did not know where to go, but as they walked along they saw a large mound of earth in front of them. "What is this?" asked First Man. "It was not here when we came this way some time ago!"

"It is a house!" exclaimed First Woman. "Someone is living here."

Just then they heard a small voice calling to them, "Come in! Come in! And see how you like our home!"

The First People walked all around the house, but nowhere could they find a door. "How can we get inside?" they called back to the person who had invited them to enter.

"On the top! On the top!" was the reply.

They all scrambled to the top of the mound and, sure enough, they found a square opening from which a notched pole protruded, and it served as a ladder for going down into the house.

"Come down the pole, that is the way to enter our dwelling," a voice directed.

So the group of First People climbed down the pole and found themselves inside a large, new home. The interior was not only one big room; it was divided into many small rooms, each serving some special purpose. There were workrooms, storerooms, sleeping rooms, and nurseries for the babies, and in every room people were busily working. Some were bringing seeds to fill the storerooms, some were carrying away earth in order to make the rooms larger, and others were plastering the inside walls with clay.

"We are the Ant People," they told the visitors, "and we are sure you will like our new house. It is partly underground and partly on ground level, but the whole house is covered with earth to make it like the land on which it is built, so our enemies cannot find it easily." The First People agreed that this was a very good idea. "There is one opening in the roof, but there is also a hidden doorway facing the east where we enter through a long passageway." This, too, seemed to be a very good idea. "The shape of our house and of the inside floor is circular because that is the shape of the sun and of the full moon," explained the Ant People. "And we have rooms under the floor for storing our winter's supply of food and our other valuables."

The First People nodded at each other and said, "This house will not blow away and the rain cannot harm it." They were pleased with the plastered walls and the hard clay floor. "Now we know how to build the houses in which we wish to live!" They thanked the Ant People and First Woman gave them bright pebbles of all colors to place on the roofs of their homes.

The First People decided to travel no further, but to return to their own mountains and make use of all the knowledge they had gained from all the people they had visited. First Woman said, "Our houses will be round, as all the homes we have visited have been that shape. We will build the walls of logs and make them higher than our heads, as do the eagles and the beaver. We will have a dome-shaped roof with an opening to the sky, and we will have a doorway facing east so the sun can waken us in the morning. Our floors and walls will be plastered with adobe mud like the homes of the swallows. Then," she added, "when it is finished we will cover the house with earth to resemble the land all about us, and we will hang a woven blanket over the doorway."

Everyone was satisfied that this plan of house building would make a very comfortable dwelling which would be cool in summer and warm in the winter. So this is the way Navaho hogans are built to this very day.